To Levi

CW00405163

YOU'RE IN THE NAVY NOW

H.M.S Edinburgh

A teenage recruit sees front-line action in WWII

From Ala A. Higgins

14 Thug. 2015

ALAN HIGGINS

YOU'RE IN THE NAVY NOW

A teenage recruit sees front-line action in WWII

ALAN HIGGINS

EDITED BY GLENN BOOKER

MEMOIRS
CIRENCESTER

Published by Memoirs

MEMOIRS
PUBLISHING

1A The Market Place Cirencester Gloucestershire GL7 2PR
info@memoirsbooks.co.uk | www.memoirspublishing.com

You're in the Navy now

ISBN: 978-1-86151-064-8

ACKNOWLEDGEMENTS

I wish to thank Glenn Booker for his time in converting my handwritten memories into text and in choosing relevant photographs. I would also like to acknowledge the help of my daughter Susan for coordinating the communication between myself, Glenn and Memoirs Publishing.

This book is dedicated to the brave seamen of *HMS Edinburgh* and all those who served on the "Convoys to Hell" who were not as fortunate as I was and did not survive.

Early days in Barry

I was born at Number 28 Burlington Street, Barry Dock, on November 25th 1923, one of seven children. It would have been eleven if the quads born 18 months after me had been able to survive. Alas, they lived only for about eighteen days.

As a young lad of that period, the 1920s and the 30s, one had to make one's own pleasures such as the street games 'Bumbarino', 'Hecky Go Jump', 'Mob' and so on. At twelve years old these pleasures would include lighting fires on the patch of (as then) un-built-on ground at the end of the street and roasting potatoes. When workmen were laying the huge gas mains between the gasworks and the gasometer on the Moors we used to collect and melt the lead wool sealing material, melting it in tin cans, then pouring it into mud moulds and imprinting them with our initials.

Another summer treat was swimming naked with the rest of the Burlington Street gang – Larry Clements, Lofty Marsh, Tommy Baker and others at Tom Edge, a reservoir at the east end of the New Docks (Number Two Dock). This pleasure was interrupted by the sight of PC Trigg, the docks policeman, which sent us scampering across the surrounding fields.

To augment the family income I used to sell the *South Wales Echo*. I picked it up at five o'clock at Barry Dock Station. Then at 5 pm I used to run up Dock View Road, Thompson Street and Holton Road shouting 'EK WEE HO!' I received threepence per dozen sold and it was a great pleasure to give my mother a few shillings a week to add to the meagre pay my dad earned as a coppersmith for a few days work in the Graving Dock.

At Holton Road School I remember Pop Humphries, a veteran of the First World War, a strict but humorous teacher. He would call out one boy thus: 'Inigo, out you come for the caning'. That was Inigo Jones, a good boyhood friend of mine. Other boys in my class were Sydney Pycroft, Peter Luen, Jacky Batt, Ossie Evans, Billy Lovell, Ken Lee, Leonard Francis and more.

COUNTDOWN TO WAR

I left school at fourteen and worked for Ernie Webb, greengrocer, fishmonger, and seller of poultry in Holton Road. However in 1938 the clouds of war were gathering and rather belatedly the Government decided to prepare for the worst by building hangars at RAF St Athan. This led to the town of Barry becoming the place of leave for large numbers of RAF apprentices with their different-coloured bands around their caps, the colour indicating the trade for which they were being trained.

My two older sisters became attached to a couple of sergeants and brought them home. They were Big John and Little John, a nice couple of chaps. I recall one of them bending a paper clip to the shape of an engine crankshaft to explain how an internal combustion engine worked.

At fifteen years of age my mind was made up: the RAF was my future. I caught the train to Cardiff and went to the RAF Recruiting Office, only to be rejected because of my lack of the required educational standard. Surprise, surprise - next door was the Royal Navy recruiting office and after a brief medical, an eyesight test, weighing, and a mental arithmetic test, to enlist I was given a standard form to fill in. I needed my parents' consent and a referee – this was Councillor Bill Butcher from Coigne Terrace. After posting the form to the Admiralty I received a letter telling me to wait until a boy's class had vacancies.

SIGNING ON WITH THE NAVY

On September 18th 1939 I was told by letter to go 120 Victoria Road, Bristol, near Temple Meads Station, for a final medical examination, which I passed. I then went by train to Plymouth, then Devonport, to formally join the Royal Navy.

I recall that when the train was at Newton Abbott in Devon a man entered our compartment with a local newspaper. The front page headline was not a good omen: '600 Men Lost on HMS Courageous'. The *Courageous* was an aircraft carrier which had been sunk the day before. When we arrived at the main barracks at HMS *Drake* there were hundreds of men, women and children scouring the 'missing' lists looking for names of their loved ones.

We spent the day and following night at the barracks, then the next morning I signed a contract to serve for twelve years from the date of my eighteenth birthday. I was still just fifteen years old.

We then went across a creek to HMS *Impregnable*, a boys' training ship, where we were issued with all our kit and hammocks. Sailors are fully equipped to be sent anywhere, with all clothes and bedding. All our clothes had to be marked with our names in red silk chain stitched in our dark woollens, white cotton in our blue serge and black cotton in our duck suits (canvas). At that time I had no idea what department I was to join: gunnery, engine room, torpedoes, or communications branch.

One day an officer came to the class where I was being taught knots and splices and asked if any boys were interested in communications. I volunteered and after a brief test on maths was accepted.

THE ISLE OF MAN

Six of us boys were sent by train to Liverpool, where we were to catch the Isle of Man ferry *Rushen Castle*. The signal school was in Douglas; it was a holiday camp previously called Cunninghams and then renamed HMS *St George*, a boys' Royal Navy ship. There I was taught the Morse Code at 22 words per minute (about two letters or figures per second); semaphore and flashing, which was Morse with a lamp and dozens of flags and pendants, their names, colours, shape and their meanings, singly or in groups.

We used to perform squad drill using flags. For example 'Quick march!' was flags G and 4, which indicated four miles per hour. Turning was a blue pendant, which meant all turn together 90 degrees to starboard or right turn etc.

We were marched to Balacameen School, where we were taught physics and maths. As I had left school at fourteen my education was very poor with the result that I was the slowest ship in the convoy, but I just passed all the exams, although I was bottom of the class in trigonometry and electricity.

The cooks at the camp were civilian and the food was awful. We were given a shilling a week out of our five shillings and threepence pay, so once a fortnight, during the afternoon, I would go to Woolworths in Douglas and buy three pennyworth of broken biscuits. From my pay I made a weekly allowance of two and six to my home. I was told that our family had a nice cooked dinner every Thursday from that money. My brother Wyndham collected this allotment from the post office in Weston Hill, Barry, submitting my official number D/JX164059. He still remembers the number to this day.

HOSPITAL TREATMENT

I interrupted my course with a hospital break of about ten days with Dhoby Itch. To explain: I was getting 'confirmed' and the Padre would take us cycling around the Isle of Man for recreation. My underpants were rough wool and my trousers rough serge, so my inner legs became severely chafed and began to weep. The only cure was an application of some ointment called Whitefields, which stung but cured the itch.

The hospital visit put me back a few classes, so my year's course was prolonged. The system was thus: although the course was dual, both signals and telegraphy, one could choose which. Some boys wanted to be signalmen and some wanted to be telegraphists. I chose the latter. Having passed the tests, on completion I was sent back to HMS *Drake* at Devonport just in time for the blitz which destroyed the centre of Plymouth and wiped out Devonport shopping centre.

With an RAF driver we went to various damaged houses and took the furniture which had survived either to Home Park (Plymouth Argyle's football ground) or to some of the occupants' friends or relatives. Sadly, after storing hundreds of pieces of furniture in the grandstand, an incendiary bomb burnt it and all the rescued furniture to the ground!

A ship of my own

It was now April 1941. At Devonport all of us boys who had completed training were waiting anxiously for ships to join. By chance I heard one boy complaining rather loudly that he'd got HMS *Edinburgh*, a cruiser, and he wanted a smaller ship such as a destroyer. I asked him if I could ask the Chief Petty Officer whether I could have the *Edinburgh* instead of him. The CPO phoned the 'Detailed for Drafting Office' and found out that I could. At 7.30 pm the next morning, with kitbag and hammock, I joined the train at the Barrack Railway station and was on my way to Scapa Flow via Thurso, the most northerly port on the mainland of the British Isles.

I was billeted in a church for a few days, where I slept in the pews and lived on corned beef sandwiches. A drifter then took me, very seasick, across the Pentland Firth to Scapa Flow, where I was billeted on the *Iron Duke* a First World War battleship with 13.9 inch guns. She was an accommodation ship, being too old for active duty. Later

I was transferred to the *Dunline Castle*, a liner converted into a large accommodation ship.

PUTTING TO SEA

After a few days I heard that my ship was due. I waited excitedly and anxiously for her to arrive. HMS *Edinburgh* was a 10,000 ton, six-inch gun cruiser, and as she came through the boom I could see from all the salt encrusted about her that she really was a sea-going vessel. HMS *Edinburgh* had been mentioned in the *Daily Express* as 'Cruiser X'. She had steamed 125,000 miles in 16 months, equivalent to five times around the globe. She was to be at sea almost all the time, returning to harbour only to refuel and take on stores.

I was transported aboard from the accommodation ship to become part of the ship's company and billeted on the boys' mess deck, where I would live with a dozen or so other boys. There were four telegraphist boys: Noble-Partridge (Cardiff); two from Northern Ireland, 'Blondie' Ratcliffe from 'up north' and Jack Thwait, who was a boy signalman. The remainder were gunnery or seaman boys, including a boy from Llanelli and Jack Jenkins from Neath, near Swansea.

Although I was a trained telegraphist, my job in my watch-keeping was decoding messages transmitted 24 hours a day to the entire Home Fleet. The messages came in four-figure groups which had to be subtracted (without carrying) from four-figure groups on a one-time code pad. The answers would then be looked up in the Fleet Signal Book, which contained the alphabet, geographical places, a dictionary and names and phrases relevant to naval procedures etc.

Sometimes a word was not in the FSB and had to be spelt out. For example 'cutaneous anthrax' had been contracted by a Royal Marine serving on a ship employed on east coast convoy duties. Of the sixteen letters in that disease name, each letter had a four-figure group, which meant 80 subtractions from the one-time pad, and each completed word resulted in 80 'lookings-up' in the aforementioned FSB.

'TEAPOT LID OVERBOARD!'

Sometime during the watch, at 2 am say, I would have to make the tea or coffee for the entire watch in different offices all over the ship. So off I'd go all along the passage through three or four watertight doors, unclipping them and re-clipping each one, with their six clips. Then I would duck under the hammocks to our mess, where I would put the tea strainer into the one-gallon tin teapot before putting into it two handfuls of tea or coffee. Next, up the ladder I would go to the galley to put in boiling water. I would return down the ladder to the mess to put into the tin pot one tin of evaporated milk, then two handfuls of brown sugar. Then I'd proceed back to the main office through all the doors and again dish out the tea or coffee.

Pouring the tea was an art form, especially when the ship was rolling, for if poured with the roll the tea would rush out all over the recipient, whereas against the roll nothing would come out of the spout unless the pot was tipped fully.

Then it was back along the same passage with the clipping and un-clipping of the watertight doors, then a cautionary look onto the upper deck where we had a lone operator, a free Frenchman, in the Direction Finding Office on the starboard side. When the ship rolled to port the starboard side was safe to dash to the DFO door before the reversed role filled the upper deck with water. This was particularly hazardous in a North Atlantic gale during the pitch black morning. After pouring the lone operator his tea, you waited again for the port side roll seaward, then dashed out to climb two ladders to the Remote Control Office behind the bridge. I recall one night when the wind was so strong it blew the lid of the teapot into the sea. To top it all the operators would moan that the tea or coffee was not hot!

After serving the tea I would return to my decoding work and carry on to the end of my watch. Then it was back to my hammock for a sleep and break from my seasickness until 7.30 am and breakfast, if I felt like it.

After that I had to scrub out one of our five wireless offices. The one I hated the most was the Remote Control Office behind the bridge, because here was the most violent rolling during a gale. I used to spew and retch into the scrubbing bucket as it went to and fro, then dip my scrubber or cloth into the bucket to carry on the cleaning. Sometimes during my sickness ordeal I'd almost finish the job when the bucket would tip over and I would have to mop up all over again. So that was my lot aboard the Edinburgh.

ICELAND

After being picked up on joining Edinburgh, we sailed to a fjord at the northwest corner of Iceland, where, after oiling and storing, we went on our normal patrol, which was covering the Denmark Straits, the sea between Iceland and Greenland. Our mission was to detect and report – and capture, if possible – any German merchant ships or warships attempting to enter or leave the North Atlantic.

Besides the monotony of the patrol the weather could often be rough, even on occasions hurricane force. One time we were with a ten thousand ton cruiser, HMS *Kent*, and although steaming six knots just to keep our bows into the storm, I saw her keel as the bows left the water, and realised ours must have been doing likewise.

The Home Fleet came on this occasion searching for the German 'pocket battleship' *Admiral Scheer*. How the men on the small destroyers coped with all the violent movements of this hurricane I just didn't know, though I found out later when I joined one of them. Most astounding was seeing the 33,000-ton battleship HMS *Rodney* as she appeared to be diving, burying all her long bows and triple 16-inch turrets under the sea, only to emerge ponderously in a flurry of foam and sea. She looked almost as though she were diving like a submarine.

There were other calmer times when we went to investigate the ice cap. For days we cruised through pack ice when the only sea visible was at the stern where we had broken through the ice leaving a trail of broken ice floes. This gave me some peace of mind, as I realised that U-Boats could not operate in such conditions.

MALTA AND THE MEDITERRANEAN

This pattern of patrols was repeated time and again until we did our first Malta convoy in July 1941. The pleasure of the blue calm seas around Gibraltar and the safety of harbour, shops, bars etc. were beyond recall. A few days of this heaven was spoilt by the arrival of the MV *Pasteur*, a French troopship carrying hundreds of British soldiers, the Lancashire Fusiliers, with a few hundred boarding us and the escorts and the merchant ships that were due for a Malta convoy. Malta lies about a thousand miles east of Gibraltar and sixty miles south of Sicily, where a large number of enemy aircraft were based.

Our job, with the aircraft carrier HMS *Ark Royal* and the battlecruiser HMS *Renown*, five other cruisers and several destroyers, was to escort five merchant ships to Malta. A ruse to fool the enemy was attempted; we sailed, in daylight, into the Atlantic. Then, during the night we reversed course and sailed through the Straits of Gibraltar, supposedly undetected, for Malta. Not a hope, for we passed by dozens of Spanish fishing boats, most with German spies aboard. At that time Spain was a firm ally of Nazi Germany.

BATTERED FROM THE AIR

The first day passed fairly peacefully, but on the second day we were attacked by Italian high-level bombers. The third day it was everything from dive-bombers and high-level bombers to torpedo bombers. The *Ark Royal* carried fighter aircraft, but although they did a good job, they were old-fashioned Fairey Fulmars, two-seater planes, not as effective as Spitfires or Hurricanes. The destroyer *Fearless* was sunk and the cruiser *Manchester* badly damaged by a torpedo; a merchant ship was torpedoed but managed to survive and make it to Malta. Other destroyers were damaged but managed to keep on fighting.

Below decks in the transmitter room where I went during action stations, there was food for thought during a torpedo attack; one hit and that would be it for us, as we were battened down in the bottom of the ship.

The night before we arrived in Malta we were attacked by E-Boats and sank two of them. On arrival in Grand Harbour, Malta, we felt very proud. The Maltese were crowding the battlements and cheering us as we had arrived just in time - as the island was virtually out of food and oil.

Four days later we were back in Gibraltar. From here we took a convoy of fast troop ships to Cape Town, South Africa. That was a cruise, as it was quiet with lots of sunshine. The people of South Africa entertained the ship's company with lashings of fruit, parties and, for me and another boy, Jack Jenkins from Neath, an invitation to stay at the house of a lawyer who, with his wife, took us on various trips including one to the Table Mountain. Here we had tea consisting of fresh cakes, honey, and cream and scones!

A MYSTERIOUS BAG OF FRUIT

As boys we were only allowed to stay off the ship until 6 pm so I was on the last train from Cape Town to the ship at Simonstown, sharing the compartment with another boy, 'Blondie' Ratcliffe. He had had too much to drink and dropped off to sleep. I shook him awake at Simonstown and asked him what he wanted to do with his large brown bag containing mixed fruit, including fresh pineapples. After we had boarded the Edinburgh I tried to give him the parcel, but he belligerently refused to accept it, saying: 'It's not mine!'

Next morning an irate able-bodied seaman came to our mess deck asking for a large bag of fruit which he'd given to Blondie to bring back to the ship. He had expected to bring this parcel to the UK for his family. (The chance of him seeing his family in the near future was somewhat remote, anyway.) Of course, the boys had eaten it all. He was very angry!

LUCKY CHOICE

After ten days of paradise we were on our way back to Gibraltar to join another Malta convoy. Heading north, we called in at Freetown in Sierra Leone in West Africa and, behold, my elder brother Lewis was there serving on the battlecruiser HMS *Repulse*. Of course I paid him a visit and he asked me if I wanted to transfer to his ship. Thankfully, I refused, because six months later she was sunk by Japanese aircraft at the time of the Fall of Singapore. She had very inadequate anti-aircraft protection, a couple of eight barrelled 'Pom Poms' and some quadruple .5 inch machine guns, no match for the Japanese air force as it turned out.

My brother also said that *Repulse* was an unlucky ship for on the way down to Freetown, for while walking on the quarter-deck, two or three petty officers were suddenly washed overboard by a freak wave and drowned. Then the ordnance petty officer was crushed to death by the hydraulic mechanism of the 15-inch gun breech during an inspection.

This convoy was similar to the first, except that the battleship HMS *Prince of Wales* was with us this time. We had the usual air attacks, but the Italian fleet came on the scene to join the attack: two battleships, five cruisers and a number of destroyers. At first the Prince of Wales went after the Italians, aided by two destroyers. At about 28 knots she looked a fine sight, but she was not fast enough, so *Edinburgh* and the cruiser HMS *Sheffield* left us behind to do battle. We were really speeding, but as the *Sheffield* edged past us she signalled: 'Do you want a tow?' Now we were the flagship, so when we crawled past her at about 32.5 knots we replied: 'No, do you?'

The Italian Fleet had no intention of engaging us – their plan was to draw the escorts away from the convoy. We two pursuing cruisers – the *Sheffield* and the *Edinburgh* – were just, however, within range and a few 15" shells hit the sea about 400 yards from us, sending up fountains of water which were quite impressive.

The attack by the Italian surface forces worked in so far as their aircraft succeeded, due to reduced anti-aircraft fire, in torpedoing the battleship HMS *Nelson* and sinking a merchant ship. Although the *Nelson* had been hit in the bows she was not seriously damaged. After delivering the remaining merchant ships to Malta we went back to Gibraltar and resumed our patrol duties off Iceland.

A CONVOY FOR RUSSIA

In December we escorted our first Russian convoy, PQ 6. At that time of the year the convoying was not too bad with regard to aerial attack because of the almost total darkness, but even with very little daylight we were still shadowed by Focke Wulfe Condors which were guiding U-Boats onto the convoy by radio.

All went well until we were nearly at Murmansk, when a Junkers JU 87 (Stuka) attack hit an American ship. Fortunately the bomb did not explode, so she completed the discharge of her cargo. During the attack the destroyer HMS *Echo* lost two men overboard who, because of the icy water, did not survive the few minutes it took for the *Echo* to rescue them. Both seamen died of hypothermia.

For Christmas dinner we had a half tin of Maconachies' steak and kidney pudding and two spoonfuls of rice. After successfully escorting a returning convoy, QP4, we arrived back in Iceland and resumed patrolling the seas between Iceland and Denmark, the Denmark Straits.

In February 1942 we sailed to South Shields on the Tyne for maintenance. This period in dock came at an appropriate juncture, as there had been some previous minor unrest on board in the shape of an 'L for Leave' campaign with the slogans appearing on the ship's bulkheads in pencil. Most of the crew, although serving in the Home Fleet, had not been home for twelve to eighteen months, while some of their families had been suffering in air raids.

The South Shields docking allowed us a week's leave. I enjoyed mine with my family and had a night in Cardiff with two other Edinburgh men, with my mother, Colin Berryman from the Valleys and his mother, and a Cardiffian, Noble-Partridge. Sadly, Colin was killed later on HMS *Trinidad* on his way back home after the events dealt with in the next chapter.

TO RUSSIA WITH STEEL

We returned to patrolling the Denmark Straits before preparing for PQ14, another convoy bound for Russia. We also carried steel plating for the repair of the cruiser Trinidad, which during a previous attack on some German warships had torpedoed herself because of a faulty gyroscope in one of her torpedoes, with tragic consequences.

PQ14 was a similar experience, except that the air and U-Boat attacks were even more severe. The convoy lost four merchant ships and a few vessels turned back because of damage caused by ice floes and bad weather.

The sinking of the *Edinburgh*

I had joined HMS *Edinburgh* in April 1941. Between monotonous patrols of the Denmark Straits, which separate Iceland and Greenland, on the lookout for blockade runners, *Edinburgh* did two Malta convoys and one Russian convoy. The Malta convoys had all the excitement of air attacks and at one time, together with HMS *Sheffield*, we chased the Italian fleet, which contained at least two battleships. The Russian convoy of December 1941 had been marred by the loss of two seamen from the destroyer HMS *Echo* who had gone overboard during a Stuka attack at the entrance of the Kola inlet. Although the *Echo* had immediately turned to pick up the seamen, the combination of heavy winter duffle coats and the bitter cold of the sea made this a futile gesture. I remember spending Christmas day in the Kola Inlet and I can't think of a more desolate place for such a festive occasion.

On April 29th we had, ironically, left the convoy because of U-Boat activity, as a cruiser is too big a target to participate in anti-U-Boat operations.

TO RUSSIA WITH GOLD

After a short time in the Kola Inlet waiting for a return convoy to the United Kingdom to assemble we took on five tons of Russian gold, payment for armaments supplied by the USA and the UK. We then sailed to escort convoy QP11 back to Britain.

Just after 4 pm the afternoon watch was settling down for tea, which was tea, bread and butter and jam. Because of the wartime complement space was at a premium, and as I was perpetually seasick I needed a place to lie down whenever I was off watch.

I vividly remember to this day lying on top of some clothes lockers when a voice from the mess deck, belonging to a telegraphist called Brown, informed me that I was poaching his billet. Just then there was a terrific explosion and a blinding flash, followed by darkness. Then I heard cries from the injured and dying in the next compartment, a scant eighth-of-an-inch steel bulkhead away.

Emergency lanterns lit automatically, and the ship felt as though she was clasped in a trembling hand which was turning it over to the starboard side at a steep angle. Oil had spilled onto the cork lino and I remember being last in a queue of Royal Marines and communication ratings and unable to keep my feet on the slippery deck. I had to crawl on hands and knees, holding on to the legs of the clothes lockers to make progress. You can imagine how slowly the queue moved as, one by one, the men squeezed through the one small hatch.

A DROP IN THE OCEAN

However, after getting through the hatch and emerging on the catapult deck, a very funny incident occurred. Because of the number of men engaged in running a wartime cruiser, the Admiralty had issued an order that in the event of a ship listing to, say, the port side, the crew were to muster on the starboard side, providing an adjustment to the list (ridiculous!) I emerged on the side nearest the water and was told in no uncertain manner that my eight stone (112lb) was urgently needed on the high side of the ship. The list was so steep that I had to crawl across and up the catapult deck, where a number of men had thrown a Carley Float over the side and in their haste had forgotten to hold the line securing it to the ship. Because the ship was still under way, the Carley Float just drifted away. Not that it would have been much use, because the sea was so cold that a few minutes would have been all one could have expected to survive clinging to a raft.

Incidentally this Carley Float was intended for 80 men,

working on the principle that a number of the ship's company would already have been killed and that those who had survived could take turns either swimming or clinging to the float.

Someone asked for volunteers to fight a fire aft, but on my arrival at the scene of the fire, a bit of paintwork was making a small blaze which to me was not serious, especially in respect of the other damage. I thought we had only been hit by one torpedo amidships, just forward of the mess deck, but on going aft I could see that thirty to forty feet of stern had been blown completely away by a second torpedo and that the quarter deck had curled up like a sardine-can lid, enveloping the two six-inch gun turrets so completely that the two sets of triple guns were actually protruding through the quarterdeck, rendering them completely useless. Feeling cold, I went to a small direction-finding wireless room on the starboard side where I knew I could find a pair of overalls which I had washed and put out to dry the previous day. These helped a lot.

While on the starboard side a torpedo man fired the four 21" torpedoes into the sea to lighten that side by about eight tons. Also on that side we had our one and only lifeboat, a cutter. It was grossly overcrowded and, thanks to a warped launching gear, refused to launch. This was just as well, for I am sure this boat would not have stayed afloat with so many in it and there would have been between twenty and thirty more casualties.

The *Edinburgh* was on her own and only just buoyant. Luckily the U-Boat which has attacked us had run out of torpedoes, or it could have delivered the coup de grace. A number of men had been battened down in the next mess deck to us and I could here their cries for help. About fifty men died to create this buoyancy. All mess decks were airtight, on the principle that if air couldn't escape water couldn't get in, so preventing further flooding. However hard a course this may seem, it was a choice of either losing all 800 men or perhaps fifty, and the answer was too obvious to even consider.

THE CRIPPLED SHIP

The torpedo that hit us amidships on the starboard side had destroyed our two main wireless transmitter rooms, which left us with a small emergency transmitter in the remote control office behind the bridge. This was our only means of communication with the convoy escort. Thankfully it did what was desired of it, although it was hours before two destroyers, HMS *Forrester* and HMS *Foresight*, arrived. Without steering the ship could only limp along in one big circle – cold comfort with a U-boat lurking about. The *Edinburgh* was silent except for a deep noise from a loose part, probably the starboard propeller shafts banging against the hull; the ship's death knell.

The two destroyers were a very welcome sight, because

one had the feeling that if the *Edinburgh* did sink there was an outside chance of being picked up. Next day we were joined by two Russian destroyers which began an attempt to tow us, interrupted at times by attacks from three large German Z-Class destroyers.

On May 1st the two Russian destroyers departed, leaving two RN destroyers and one crippled cruiser at the mercy of the three German destroyers. Both our destroyers were hit, one on the bridge, killing the Captain, and for a time both the escorts were stationary on account of engine room damage. The situation changed dramatically as the three 'Z' class German destroyers returned with guns far larger than our destroyers, and we on *Edinburgh* were unable to fire our guns effectively because of the instability caused by our loss of power. After five attacks by the enemy destroyers on our three British ships – which were temporarily out of action – I remember thinking that it was safer to stand on the side from which the Germans were firing. That way the only chance of being hit was a direct hit by a shell, rather than shrapnel from an exploding shell.

FIGHTING BACK

Then there occurred an incident that made me feel very proud. Three small minesweepers, *Harrier, Gossamer* and *Hussar*, each armed with a four–inch unshielded 'pop gun', charged at the speed of 15 knots at the three powerful

German destroyers. Although they disappeared at times in a welter of German 'straddles', they emerged miraculously, it seemed, to pop away at the Germans as confidently as ever, eventually driving them away.

They came to reinforce our sorry group. Through skilled repairs the two British destroyers were again made ready for action, but unfortunately the captain and some other members of one of the destroyers were killed by a direct hit on the bridge and engine rooms. The other destroyer also had casualties, but I am pleased to say that her captain survived to become an Admiral; he still attends our annual reunion of survivors.

The situation looked brighter, and with the two British destroyers towing and steering *Edinburgh*, which was, incredibly, still using her engines and one propeller, the group began making for Murmansk.

TRAPPED

We had reckoned without the return of the German destroyers. As the Russian ships had left for refuelling, we were again in a desperate state. I remember being below decks when an explosion from a third torpedo threw me unconscious to the deck among the dust, falling pipes and vent shafts. After regaining consciousness and gathering my wits, I tried moving my arms, then my legs and finally my back, and to my relief found I was OK apart from my dazed condition. I was alone and lying at the foot of a ladder with an armoured hatch above me shut tight; the deck outside the galley had collapsed.

I looked for a way out, but the hatch was impossible to open. The way forward was blocked and the only way out seemed to be aft. So through the gloom and dust I began feeling my way back out. Just as I began to move aft the Chief Petty Officer, a cook named Gray from Cwmbran, came out of the galley just in front of me. In the gloom he just vanished into the depths where the deck had collapsed, so he lost his life.

I was now trapped, and I remember thinking, 'What silly idiot closed the hatch?' Closing it was quite useless. I was on the upper deck which, if that had flooded, would have meant the ship was sinking anyway.

It was not long before the hatch opened and a face peered through it and asked, 'What are you doing down here?' In retrospect I have thought of dozens of answers, but at the time all I was wanted was to get out into the open.

After the fashion of channel swimmers, I went to the hangars and applied liberal dollops of thick grease about my ears and hands. I thought I would have a better chance of surviving if I did go into the water.

The ship was settling deeper, but fate had been kind to her as the third torpedo had hit on the exact opposite side to one of the first torpedoes, and the damage was not quite so severe, although she must have been near to breaking in half. We were carrying a number of wounded merchant seamen and our Admiral, Stuart Bonham Carter, ordered two minesweepers alongside. I vaguely remember the Russian gunboat being present also. HMS *Gossamer* came alongside first and took off most of the *Edinburgh* crew on the starboard side, including the wounded, and some merchant seamen who were being taken back to the UK, and then she left.

SINKING THE *SCHOEMANN*

On the port side I recall a coder by the name of Kneebone helping me with one stretcher case, a Lascar seaman who could not move. The *Edinburgh* and *Harrier* were yawing apart and I could imagine the poor chap's feelings as he was passing over the gap between the two ships. I am glad to say we did not lose a man in these operations. At one stage Kneebone and I were carrying a stretcher across the flight deck and our forward six-inch opened up. The shock was such that I almost dropped the stretcher.

On the port bow I could see a German destroyer firing on us. We hit her and set her on fire. She was the *Hermann Schoemann* and she sank a little later. A victory for the *Edinburgh*! I remember seeing the ship disappear, making smoke, but it was only in the 1990s that I read that she had been sunk.

The order to abandon ship was given and I was

surprised to find that there were very few of us left aboard. I went on the *Harrier*, as did Admiral Bonham-Carter and the captain, Hugh Faulkner. I was one of the last to leave.

FAREWELL TO THE SHIP

We made several attempts to scupper the *Edinburgh*. First, we dropped depth charges beneath her, then we fired point blank into her magazines. I remember seeing the 'Pom Pom' and 'ready use' four-inch shell magazines blowing up, but she seemed almost indifferent to our efforts to sink her.

A few of the crew prepared to ask the Admiral if we could go back aboard, as the *Edinburgh* seemed unsinkable, and after all a sailor gets very attached to his ship. However, the thought of a humble telegraphist approaching a Rear Admiral was too great to contemplate, so I stayed on the stern and watched while one of the destroyers delivered the coup-de-grace. I learned later that the Rear Admiral had also considered re-boarding, because if the Germans had towed the *Edinburgh* away with all that gold on board it would have been a disaster. Luckily one of our destroyers had a torpedo left. This had misfired during an earlier attack upon the German destroyers.

Now the ship had been hit by two torpedoes amidships and one aft, which meant that she was fairly sound forward and in the engine and boiler rooms, but flooded elsewhere. When the final torpedo, fired by our own destroyer, hit her in the boiler room, a cavernous space stretching from the keel to the upper deck with no watertight deck levels, she went down very quickly, in a few minutes, stern first, vertically until the bows were perpendicular. Then she came back and 'curtsied,', but when the water level reached her forward gun turrets, she slide quietly out of sight.

OUT FOR THE COUNT

On the *Gossamer* I remember going below, where neat rum was being issued from a stained teacup. At first, being teetotal, I tentatively sipped the rum, but as this drew forth groans of anger from shipmates I gulped the tot down and went forward in a daze. I must have looked a pretty sight being plastered with that grease as a protection against the cold.

As I was teetotal and very hungry, the naval rum had a devastating effect upon me. I remember sitting on the messdeck stool and playing cards with three other men. The cards all looked the same colour – no blacks or reds – all plum red! Then I collapsed on the deck and lay there unconscious...

The action had lasted for about three days, as the Edinburgh sank on May 2nd, 1942. I suppose the thought of dying affects different people in different ways, but all I could think of at the time was how to die quickly by gulping in sea water, and wondering how my parents would take the news. On this voyage, Edinburgh was carrying a 4.5-long-ton (4,570 kg) consignment of gold bullion, intended as partial payment for Allied supplies to the USSR. The 465 gold ingots, carried in 93 wooden boxes, were in the armoured bomb-rooms on the starboard side, near the first torpedo's impact point. At the time, the estimated worth of the bullion was about £1.5 million sterling.

Thanks to the value of that cargo, that wasn't the last the world saw of the *Edinburgh*. Although the wreck was designated as a war grave, the British Government was anxious to recover the gold – not just because of its value, but because there was a growing fear that the wreck might be looted, or salvaged by the Soviet Union. The salvage rights went to Jessop Marine, and in April 1981, the survey ship *Dammtor* found the wreck at a depth of 245 metres (800 ft). The *Dammtor* took detailed film of the wreck which allowed the divers to plan a salvage operation, studying her sister ship HMS Belfast to asses the layout. Later that year salvage operations began in earnest and eventually all but five of the ingots were recovered. The gold was now worth £45m.

Polyarno, Russia

Some hours later I was awakened by a Petty Officer, who ordered me to go onto the snow-covered jetty at Polyarno, where the ship's company was being mustered to check for those who had been lost in action. The Paymaster captain read out the names from the pay lists and any non-response was followed by a few questions to confirm whether or not the sailor could have survived. Thirty-seven were defined as 'lost'. The eventual death toll was 56 ratings and two officers.

The captain then gave a speech and congratulated all of us on our past performances on *Edinburgh*. He promised to have us home in five days! So, with a blinding headache and feeling thoroughly rotten, I boarded the trawler *Silja* and sailed to Vaenga, further up the Kola Inlet.

Hundreds of our survivors marched through the deep snow attired in all manner of clothes, looking like Napoleon's army retreating from Moscow. After about an hour we arrived at a group of long wooden huts, which were warmed by large wood-burning pot-bellied stoves. There were rows of two-tiered wooden platforms of four-inch rough planks: our beds. We would wake up in the morning with lines on our bodies where the planks had bent and sometimes pinched one's skin.

FISH EYE SOUP

We were fed twice a day on a few slices of black bread together with an enamel bowl of watery soup or a mash of rice, corn or oats. Sometimes a fish eye would stare at you from the soup. After a few days when we only nibbled the bread or had a few spoonfuls of the mashed corn, hunger took over and removed all feelings of queasy stomachs. After that we ate all that was put out for us.

We were stuck in the camp in Veanga because of the PQ17 disaster. The Royal Navy escorts had left the convoy to disperse and fend for itself, because of the belief that the German battleship *Tirpitz* was at sea and in the area. This left most of the abandoned merchant ships prey to the German Luftwaffe and U-Boats and led to the cancellation of further convoys to Russia. This was why some of us were left stranded in this camp at Vaenga on a semi-starvation diet.

Life was pretty boring at Vaenga Camp. I can remember quite clearly the days when one would dream of fish and chips or bacon and eggs while one's empty stomach would roll and rumble.

AN UNEXPECTED FEAST

One day I was a lucky guest at a wonderful supper on one of the destroyers in Vaenga Bay - lucky because of a million-to-one coincidence that followed a small kindness on my part the previous Christmas. On Christmas Day 1941 on *Edinburgh* I had been approached by two seamen from HMS *Echo* or HMS *Escapade* ('E' Class destroyers) which were tied up alongside, and asked to buy them a set of playing cards from our canteen; it was larger and had a great deal more stock than the canteens on their destroyers. Unfortunately for them *Edinburgh*'s canteen had also been out of playing cards, but happily for the destroyer men I had two small packs of cards, which I had given them. They were very grateful and their gratitude paid dividends when we met six months later.

In Vaenga Bay these two aforementioned destroyers arrived unexpectedly and invited a small number of *Edinburgh* survivors, maybe twenty, to a supper. My name was picked out of a cap containing 400 names. The mess deck to which I was invited was the mess deck of two card-playing seamen. My payback was a lovely cooked supper of roast potatoes, pork and so on, followed by a gorgeous 'figgy duff' with custard. They also gave me packets of biscuits and bars of chocolate. This was one of those rare occasions where one good turn deserves another. It was a million-to-one chance to have my name picked from a hat in the camp containing hundreds of other names, and then on top of that to have landed on the mess table of the two recipients of my previous kindness!

A few months later I was transferred to a 'Y' radio station out on the hills above Polyarno. Here German-coded radio traffic between Petsamo in Finland and Kirkenes in Norway was intercepted. We would then recode the German code into our code and send it to England (to Bletchley Park, although we did not know that at the time.) There it would be deciphered by the Enigma cipher machines.

A number of memorable events took place there. On a lovely afternoon in the height of summer, a squad of armed Russian women parked outside our station. After divesting themselves of some of their clothing they washed their underwear in a small pond directly beneath our windows. As our windowpanes were somewhat dirty we were able to observe the ladies without being observed ourselves, which was just as well as they were all armed with Tommy guns!

The second incident took the form of a visit to the station by Rear Admiral Bevan, the Senior British Naval Officer North Russia. Noticing my sockless feet, he personally brought me two pairs of his own socks which had been knitted by his wife. His name was sown inside them in red silk thread.

NARROW ESCAPE

The third incident was almost my last day on earth. Six Junkers 88s bombed our station this way and that way. Although there was no direct hit I do recall lifting myself off the floor and looking out the window at the same time as a bomb blew up behind a massive boulder. If that rock had not been there to take some of the blast I would have been killed. As it was, the roof was blown off and the Y Station sagged in all directions.

But there's always a funny side to these situations. As I ran from the station, accompanied by a telegraphist from Tenby who to protect himself from the fall-out had a galvanised bucket over his head, I was brought up short by a Russian soldier pointing his rifle and bayonet at me. He warned me that I was not to go near his 30-gallon drum of something or other. Despite my pleas that I was an 'Angliski matrosk'(English sailor) and 'on his side' he became even more menacing by pulling back the bolt on his rifle. Prudently, I ran back to the Y Station, zig-zagging just in case he fired at me, which he did not, thankfully!

When I got back to the ruined station I was met by an Irish stoker named Michael emerging from the wreckage apparently covered in blood but laughing his head off. The rest of us were very concerned about Paddy, but on closer inspection we realised the cause of his hilarity. A carton of tins of damsons had been stored in the roof of the building and when Paddy had been sheltering in the boiler room this carton had been smashed by the Nazi bomb, spraying damson juice all over him!

HMS MARNE

The Y Station was destroyed, so at Polyarno I joined the destroyer HM *Marne* as a passenger, bound hopefully for the UK. However, we sailed for Archangel and spent some time there, as after the PQ17 disaster sea traffic between Britain and North Russia had virtually ceased.

I believe that apart from escorting a small convoy through the Kara Sea to the Gulf of Ob we did little else in Archangel but stay alongside. The *Marne* was low on food and ammunition, and we were rationed, as I remember, to two slices of corned beef a day and some ship's biscuits, which were like concrete, though there was plenty of tea, sugar and milk as well as some occasional chocolate from the canteen.

To supplement my diet I would daily visit the International Club in Archangel in the hope that there might be a meal going. I was successful on two occasions: on the first I was served a bowl of noodle soup and during the second I was given a large plate of white crab meat. Given the dire position that Soviet Russia was in, I admit that I was fortunate to have been served at all.

While walking to the Intourist Club I used to pass

through a park on the banks of the River Divina. In the park were rows of stone statues of naked figures, men and women. Their private parts were painted in graffiti, which made them even more erotic. As well as the statues I met an interesting flesh-and-blood character, an old man who was playing an accordion made from a Sunlight soap box which still carried its blue and red company motifs. On finding out that I was an 'Angliski matrosk' he played and sang to me a very old 1920s song, with the title 'How do you do, do, Mr Brown?' He said he knew my hometown of Barry very well as he had been an engineer on Russian ships bringing pit props to south Wales for the coal mines. Small world.

Archangel, and a date with a difference

On my visits to the International Club I met Liza, who was one of several girls known officially as hostesses. She could speak a little English, so I tried to pick up a few Russian phrases from her. One day she asked me if I would like to meet her married sister and newborn baby. I said I would love to, and we agreed a meeting after she had finished her shift at the Club.

On the day we walked to the outskirts of Archangel along the wooden sidewalks to a large communal wooden building which housed several families. On entering a large room housing a substantial iron stove and big metal trough we were met with stares from one man, and a belligerent demand: 'Second Front, da?'

At that time the Russians were at a very critical point in the war and they wanted the UK and the USA to lift some of the pressure from them by opening a Second

Front in France, so the Germans would withdraw some of their troops from the Russian Front. This 'Second Front, da?' was quite a common challenge to all the British in north Russia.

I was led by Liza through a curtain to a tiny room containing a wooden bunk, table and a single chair. Sitting on the bunk nursing a baby was Liza's young sister, who had painstakingly laid the table with a small pattern table runner, a glass of vodka and a plate with one slice of black bread covered with yak butter. The sister offered me the plate with a nice little smile, but when she saw that I was about to refuse it she gave me a look of extreme disappointment. Bear in mind that the food allowance was only half a pound of black bread a day and that this girl with a baby was giving me her daily ration, plus some very hard to obtain butter.

Liza broke in, urging me not to give a terrible insult to her sister and take up the offer. I did this reluctantly, pretending to enjoy every mouthful, which brought a look of joy to her sister's face. I then transformed the atmosphere by first giving to Liza's sister a bar of Rowntree's York chocolate and secondly by presenting her with a bar of Lux scented soap, wrapped in floral paper. (Soap was at a premium in Russia). This produced an amazing burst of joy and tears. (Once when having a shower in Vaenga I was given a piece of soap measuring a square inch by one eighth of an inch! It was hardly sufficient to wash my hands.)

The baby was given to Liza and I was embraced and kissed, together with loud praises from her sister.

As we were about to leave a tall, fairly well-dressed woman approached me and began questioning me in Russian. I was perplexed until she showed me surreptitiously from under her jumper a religious cross. When I acknowledged that I, too, was Christian, she kissed my hand.

On another occasion when I met Liza at the Club she again invited me to her flat. Unfortunately, while on our way to her abode the air raid sirens sounded and we spent several hours in a crowded shelter. To make it worse, by the time we left the curfew was in force, and from the shadows a blue-capped policeman appeared. He informed us in no uncertain terms that 'Ruski Dwiska' (Russian girl) should go only with 'Ruski Matrosk' (Russian sailor) and 'Angliski Matrosk' (English sailor) should go only with 'Englisk Dwiska' (English girl). Then he escorted me back to the ship, his pistol holster unbuttoned.

There is a sequel to this story. Imagine my surprise when I received a letter on 24th April 2010, almost 68 years later, from that young baby's granddaughter, Svetlana, in which she reminded me of the pleasure my short visit had given to her then young grandmother.

An eventful journey home

We finally left Archangel in September 1942, heading for Iceland. I did not relish this voyage as it would be in broad daylight, good for the U-Boats and the Luftwaffe. However, we were fortunate as a sea mist prevailed, so we reached Iceland without incident.

Then, to my dismay, instead of heading back to the UK, we loaded the *Marne* with ammunition for herself and for the HMS *Polamaries*, an anti-aircraft cruiser at Archangel. She had run out of ammo while escorting a convoy previously.

We were on our way back to Russia and I was in my usual spot on the upper deck when I heard the noise of a ship's machinery coming out of the sea mist. 'Oh God', I thought, 'the *Tirpitz*!' Thankfully, the US cruiser *Tuscaloosa* then appeared out of the mist. Together with another cruiser and three US destroyers she was on her way to Russia to pick a number of US Merchant Mariners, survivors of convoy PQ17.

A NARROW ESCAPE

Off North Cape, Norway, we three British destroyers left at speed, heading due south. All of us were finally on our way home. A few hours later action stations sounded. When the *Marne*'s crew rushed to their posts, I fell to my knees and said 'Please, God, not again.'

I was on the upper deck near the stern where the depth charges were stored ready for dropping when I saw the German minelayer the *Ulm*. We opened fire with our six 4.7 inch guns and I saw what I thought were red explosions on the German ship. 'Good' I thought. But then our shells straddled her a little later. Those red flashes were her guns firing at us!

There was a great explosion a matter of yards from where I was and a bloodstained figure staggered by. Then the *Ulm* seemed to begin making black smoke. When I saw flames I realised that she was well alight. The *Marne* went in to deliver the coup de grace, but we were overruled by the senior destroyer captain, who finished the job.

A little later a huge lifeboat came alongside, but it capsized. The ship's crew began taking the Germans out of the water, but a German Blom and Voss torpedo plane then began attacking us. As we were fairly close to the northern Norwegian coast and the German airfields, having picked about twenty-seven Germans, we beat a hasty retreat, leaving some of them still in the water.

The German shell that had hit us had killed some *Edinburgh* survivors and blown two depth charges over the side. While steaming at high speed the six dead were buried in dirty Royal Mail post bags by way of a plank over the stern. The standard Navy prayer was said.

HAUNTED BY FLASHBACKS

I arrived safely back in Scapa Flow and made the trip back to HMS *Drake* in Devonport. In my newly-issued uniform I waited for a train ticket to begin my 14 days' survivor leave. I was looking somewhat down and somewhat dispirited, I suppose. A friendly sailor approached me and asked me how long I had been 'in'. Thinking he meant barracks, I replied, 'Two days.' He thought that I had been in the Navy two days and followed up, 'Don't worry, you'll get used to it. I've been in the Navy three weeks.' I suppose he meant well. I had been 'in' for three years at that time.

When I came home to Barry I must have been suffering from what we now call post traumatic stress disorder. My nerves were a bit shot on leaving *Edinburgh* and my stress manifested itself in several ways. For example, I would stay on the upper deck of a ship as much as possible and I was always looking for a means of escape while below deck. On survivors' leave I would tell anyone who cared to listen of the terrible experiences I had had to endure: 'I was tin-fished three times, the quarterdeck wrapped itself around Y turret' and so on and so on!

On one occasion when an anti-aircraft gun fired a practice shot in Barry I ran down a back lane and crouched against back door for about an hour.

My cure and counselling occurred in a particularly odd manner. I went with a Plymouth girl on a date. We were walking along Union Street arm-in-arm and I began my personal lament. 'We were hit by two tin fish...' My young lady let go of my arm and said in an exasperated manner: 'What the hell is a tin fish?'

Suddenly I realised what a waste of time my moaning was. From that minute I was cured, which was just as well as the *Edinburgh* experience was minor compared to what was to follow in the next three years.

Combined operations

After leaving Russia I spent some time at HMS *Drake* (Devonport Naval Barracks), where I did a wireless telegraphy course to be made up to 'trained operator' which gave me a small pay rise.

During the course I was given fire-watching jobs in some big houses and offices in Plymouth. On two occasions I went out to the breakwater in Plymouth, where I helped to load supplies for Malta. The first ship to be loaded was HMS *Adventure*, a pre-war minelayer. The second ship was HMS *Welshman*. These were used because of their speed and the spacious cargo space provided by their mining decks.

ACROSS THE ATLANTIC

In February 1943 I was summoned to the Drafting Office and told to join a train at the barrack station at 8.30 the next morning, where I was to join Naval Party 239 or some number like that. I had no idea where I was going, but I finished up in Glasgow and joined the troopship MV Andes. We spent five days crossing the North Atlantic until we arrived at Halifax, Nova Scotia, where everyone was put on a southbound train.

An America-based British Petty Officer, Charles Dickens from Somerset Road, Barry, was put in charge of all the sailors bound for ships in the USA. Some were destined for landing craft, some for 'BYMs' or American-built minesweepers.

As 'Charlie' was based in Fargo Barracks in Boston he said he would make my stay in the US as long as possible. Charlie was a friend of the family and had joined the navy at the same time as my elder brother Lewis. Charlie had lost his ship, the cruiser HMS *Hermione*, in the Mediterranean earlier in the war and had been posted to America as Headquarters staff. There were a lot of patrol servicemen – trawlermen bound for the BYMs - and a lot of rowdy lads they were!

The train stopped in a siding alongside a large war factory manned by young females. Before long the windows of the factory were alive with the girls throwing out notes with their details wrapped in silver dollars or lighters, anything weighty enough to bring these notes to the ground. You can guess what happened next. Sailors jumped onto the track through the carriage windows (the doors being locked) to retrieve these notes, and it took some time for the train to be ready to continue its journey.

VIRGINIA BOUND

I arrived at Fargo Barracks in the evening, just in time for supper. What a surprise! With an aluminium tray one could help oneself to almost every kind of food imaginable. 'This is the life for me' I thought. Unfortunately it was not to be, as the following morning I was on a train bound for Norfolk, Virginia. Charlie Dickens had not got back to Fargo in time to settle me in.

Arriving at Norfolk, you can imagine my shock when I saw my landing craft. She was 160 feet long, 23-foot beam, flat bottomed, four-foot draught amidships, 250 tons and eight diesel main engines, each the size one would see on a bus. I was a chronic seasick sufferer on a 10,000 ton cruiser, so you can imagine how I fared on a 250 ton craft!

The crew numbered about 16 or 17 with two officers. There was a coxswain, leading seaman Alex Henderson (a dipsomaniac from Glasgow); able seamen Phillips, Lloyd, Wilkins, Parr etc; leading stokers Joe Pegg and Lofty Dawson; wireman Clem Bailey; a motor mechanic, MacKenzie (Port Arthur, Canada); and a few others whom I cannot now remember. The captain was Harry Collinge, Lieutenant RNVR and a Sub-Lieutenant, RNVR.

We did a few courses with the US Navy such as 'How to dress in the dark' and 'How to swim at sea through fire and flames'. Best of all was practising firing the 20 mm cannon at a drogue towed by aircraft.

About ten of the Landing Craft Infantry, Large (LCI(L)) left Norfolk in a gale for Gibraltar, my job being to receive wireless messages and then decode them. For three days I was terribly ill, not eating and being sick in a bucket, which Captain Collinge, because of the smell of the contents, asked me, politely, to empty.

BERMUDA BECKONS

On the fourth day everything changed. We arrived at Hamilton, Bermuda. The sea was calm, the water blue and I could eat and drink something. I went ashore to Hamilton and booked a night in the 'Sailors Rest'. With our poor pay we could not afford much, especially as the Americans had taken over the island under the terms of the Lend Lease Act. However, I managed to buy a lovely strawberry milkshake.

While walking about the town we were approached by a very tall civilian who said: 'I suppose you lads would like to be in London just now?' We answered 'yes' and recognising the Welsh accent we asked which part of Wales he came from. He replied that he was from Llechryd, Cardiganshire. I told him I was from Barry, to which he replied that his uncle was 'Jenkins the milk in Barry' and asked did I know him. I said no.

As we walked and talked generally he asked us if we cared to join him for a drink. We said we would, and we ended up at a pair of huge iron gates with a rather large house in the background. He then asked us if we knew where we were. My chum, John Dowden, said he knew that we were at the entrance to the home of the Governor of Bermuda, because that day he'd bought a postcard of the residence to send to his mum!

The stranger's name was Bill Williams and he was the Governor's man, an ex-policeman. Bill said that as Sir Patrick Knowles, the Governor, was away as Nassau he could entertain us to a meal and a drink. He apologised for the light supper, as the main cooks were away with the Governor. He need not have bothered to apologise - we had no cook on the landing craft, so our food was very basic.

After the meal and a few pleasant drinks, Bill let us pick a few bananas from the Governor's private stock, and so we returned to our landing craft.

ACROSS THE 'POND' AND INTO THE MED

About ten vessels formed a flotilla and we left Bermuda the next day for Gibraltar. I was given a direction-finding set to beam on any landing craft that lost its way during the night. The following morning the flotilla was re-formed after the lost sheep had been found and restored to position. We then resumed our course and after a number of 'reformations' and gatherings we finally arrived at Gibraltar.

A day or so later we sailed on to Algiers, where we were

In 1939 (aged 15) on the training ship *Impregnable*, Devonport

The boys queuing for dinner on HMS St George, Isle of Man, October 1939

Boy 1st Class Alan Higgins on leave from HMS St George, Isle of Man, December 1939

04 271 Wireless Telegraphist's course, HMS St George, Douglas Isle of Man, 1941 – I am second left front row

HMS Edinburgh

A painting by Trudy Doyle (1960) entitled 'HMS Edinburgh's last battle'

Liza, one of Stalin's hostesses,
whom I met in Archangel in 1942

Liza, a photo she sent
me in later life

The destroyer HMS *Marne*, 1942

Practice landing in Malta, 1943

LCIs en route to Elba, 1944

Wearing a borrowed battledress after mine had been ruined tending
to casualties at D-Day, June 1944

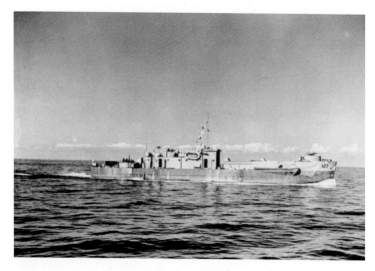

An LCI of the type I served on at D-Day

With AB Stokes (left) in 1944

On the slips in Manoel Island, Malta, 1945, for bottom scraping

Mandel Island, Sliema, Malta

LCI beached on Mandel Island, Sliema

Trying out a German helmet, Venice 1945

Resettling Greek families in Rhodes, 1945

The bodies of Mussolini and his mistress Clara Petacci
strung up by Italian partisans, 1945

Sliema on VE Day

LCI 253 in Tobruk,
1946, waiting to load
Greek mutineers to take
them to Piraeus

A memorial service in 1945/46 for the New Zealanders
who had fallen at Suda Bay

General Freyburgh at the memorial at the Suda Bay memorial service

The crew of LST 3516, on which I served in 1947 as LDG/telegraphist

Katerina Ermolina, a Russian schoolteacher who established a
Russian convoy museum at Murmansk

The crew of LCI 283 in Piraeus, Greece, 1946/7

In Suez on LST 3516, 1947

The team at Kranji Wireless Station, Singapore, 1949

The last reunion of Edinburgh survivors, at Plymouth Hoe in the late 1980s. I am right of centre holding the blue folder.

berthed near the wreck of HMS *Arrow*, a destroyer which had had the bad luck to be tied up to an ammunition ship which had blown up after a direct hit by a bomb from a German raider. All the upper works of the *Arrow* were completely blown off, leaving only the bare deck.

The Germans and Italians were still fighting the Eighth Army in the Western Desert and the Fifth Army under General Eisenhower in Algeria and Tunisia in the west, so the German air attacks on the Allies were very frequent – as we were to find out.

On the way from Algiers to the small Algerian port of Djidjelli, our flotilla of Landing Craft Infantry shot down a Junkers 88 which had the bad luck to fly between our two columns. On arrival at Djidjelli, which was to be our base, we were greeted by the sight of the burnt-out wreck of LCI(L) 7, which a few days previously had had a direct bomb hit. The nocturnal raids by the Luftwaffe were so concentrated that every night we had to anchor offshore in the bay to avoid destruction.

LEARNING ABOUT LANDING

One of the reasons for being stationed at Djedjelli was to practise troop landings, which we did on a number of occasions. The practice went as follows:

1. Slow the craft down and when about 30 yards from the beach drop the stern kedge anchor.

2. Raise the two forward ramps ready for dropping.

3. On hitting the beach or in the shallows, drop the ramps.

If you dropped the ramps too soon they would rear up and become useless. If the kedge anchor was not dropped properly or at the wrong distance the landing craft would 'broach to' on the beach sideways. This broaching actually happened once and left an LCI firmly stuck in the sand. Two destroyers were unable to get her off by themselves and it took ramming by two army tanks to literally bash her off the beach, as well as banging against a huge wooden beam which was attached to protect the ship's side.

Later we sailed to Bone. I recall a few humorous incidents on the way. As the Germans and Italians were nearing defeat in Cape Bon, they rescued as many of their soldiers as possible by Junkers 52 transport aircraft. On a lovely morning as I came up the ladder to the bridge I saw a number of these Junkers 52s overhead and mentioned the fact to the First Lieutenant. As the planes were very high he had not seen them, nor had the lookout, a young lad from Newcastle by the name of Dixon – I might add of non-University material.

'Dixon, why didn't you report those aircraft?' asked the somewhat exasperated officer. There was no response from Dixon, who was sitting on a bench just behind the bridge. The First Lieutenant said to me: 'I think he is asleep. Go and find out.' Now Dixon was wearing American sunglasses with a knob for varying the density of the lenses. When I went nose to nose I couldn't make out whether or not he was asleep as the lenses were so dark, so I told the First Lieutenant that I could not tell. The officer took off his cap and threw it at Dixon, hitting him on the head. He woke up with a start and began muttering protests.

'Dixon, you were asleep' said the officer.

'I was not,' replied the crewman.

'Then why did you not report those aircraft?' demanded the Lieutenant.

After rapidly scanning the sky and spotting the Junkers the crewman replied 'I thought you'd seen them, sir!'

There followed a stern telling off, as the responsibility of the lookout was to immediately warn the bridge of any danger. For practice the officer told the lookout to report in the future anything untoward.

The officer then said: 'Why didn't you report that motor launch approaching on the starboard quarter? Report it now!'

Rather hesitantly Dixon said: 'Ship in sight, bearing...' Then *sotto voce* he asked me: 'Where, Sparks?'

I replied, also *sotto voce*, 'Green 135'.

'Green 135, sir, ship in sight,' said Dixon. The correct answer would have been 'Ship bearing 135'.

'Dixon, 'Ship in sight bearing Green 135!'

'I know it is in bloody sight, and apart from that the bearing is now 090, try again!'

Very confused, Dixon began, 'Ship in sight...'

At this point the First Lieutenant gave up and went to the voice pipe. He said to the coxswain, who was in the wheelhouse: 'Coxswain, come up here and throw Dixon over the side, and don't let me hear the splash.'

DIXON IN DEEP - AGAIN

Another Dixon episode occurred late that same evening. I was on watch in the radio room when I heard a knock on the radio room door. In came Dixon, looking very worried. To my question 'What's up, Dixie?' he replied 'I can't tell you.'

I said 'Well then you'd better push off, then.'

'Well, I want your advice, Sparks.' He then showed me a letter and said he had just received it.

I said 'How on earth can you get a letter at sea? At this time of night?'

'Lofty Dawson, (a leading stoker,) said that he had had one as well.'

'OK, what is the trouble, then?'

'Mary is pregnant, you know, Mary who works in the chip shop?'

I replied: 'Now look Dixie, it takes a girl nine months to give birth and you left the UK fifteen months ago. So someone is pulling your leg!'

He put on his 'knew it all the time face' and left. A few minutes later he was back and said: 'But what if its twins she had? That would take twice as long.'

I left it at that!

BIZERTA AND TRIPOLI

At Bone the Luftwaffe gave the port a pounding and I was glad when we moved on to Bizerta, which was heaving with US landing craft. Walking along the banks at night I could watch half a dozen different films which were displayed on white sheets fixed to the forecastles of the LSTs. The US Navy was dry, and I sold my two bottles of navy rum to a much striped US Petty Officer for ten dollars each (£5) He made me open each bottle for a taste before the transaction because he had been caught before with bottles of cold tea looking like rum!

After a few days we sailed from Bizerta to Souse in the Gulf of Tripoli, where we waited for our first landings. We tied up alongside a phosphate jetty, where again we had to go out in the bay to anchor because of the nightly German bombing. We adopted an Eighth Army ack-ack crew and traded rum and navy cigarettes with them for their stories of the battles in which they had been engaged at Mejed El Bab.

Their sergeant was from Swansea and was very friendly. One night during a very heavy raid on Souse I saw their ack-ack gun take a direct hit. In the morning when we berthed I saw the sergeant and remarked: 'I thought that you had had it.' 'So did I,' he replied. Then he dropped his shorts and showed his backside, which was black as a result of a rock blasting him into a slit trench.

SICILY UNDER FIRE

On 11th June 1943 we took on board English soldiers for the landings at Pantelleria, Sicily, and in a short time we were waiting off the island while the US Air Force saturated it with bombs. The bombing was so intense that with binoculars we could see the bombs dropping, and in no time the island was obscured in dust.

Just before we went in to land we thwarted a German fighter-bomber attack out of the sun on the *Misoah*, a tanker which had been converted into a Landing Ship Tank. Then we witnessed a fighter dogfight above us, which resulted in the loser, a Messerschmitt 109, crashing into the sea a few yards from us. A US fighter performed a victory roll just after that.

The time came for us to go in and land. We entered the harbour without opposition, but struggled to find a place among the rubble to drop our ramps. Had there been any opposition, with the time we took we would never have made it.

As soon as our ramps were dropped hundreds of Italians, waving anything white - flags, cloths, even underwear - ran out to surrender. After we had unloaded the troops we took the Italians back to Souse to captivity. They all seemed happy that for them the war was over.

A few days later we were on our way to Lampedusa to pick up part of the Italian army which had surrendered to a Fleet Air Arm sergeant who had crash-landed his plane on the town after the island had been bombarded by the cruiser HMS *Ajax*. On the way there we witnessed an attack in full moonlight a few miles from us. A convoy was under attack from three-engine Marchetti torpedo bombers. We were creeping by when one of these planes dropped a torpedo in our direction, thankfully missing. However, our anti-aircraft fire alerted the escort of the convoy and a destroyer came charging towards us, using the Morse code challenge AA (DIDA DIDA) several times. I couldn't find the hourly-coded answer in my small cupboard on the bridge, so I used my 1000 watt ten inch lamp and spelt out: LCI 111.

The destroyer came close with all its crew at action stations and a Dartmouth-trained voice told us to buck up our ideas, as he was about to open fire on us, as at first glance we looked liked a German E-Boat. We and LCI (L) 116 went on our merry way to pick up the Italian troops at Lampedusa to take them back to Souse.

FISHING WITH GRENADES

From Lampedusa we brought back a box of Italian hand grenades coloured red. We thought they would be handy for fishing. At Souse we threw a few of them into the sea off the mole, but with no success. The Eighth Army gun crews were aghast! They told us that these red grenades were very dangerous and were apt to go off as soon as the lever was released, so we threw the remainder into the sea, still in the box.

After a few more trips to Pantelleria we set sail for Msida Creek, Malta. That night the island, which was crowded with invasion craft for the invasion of Sicily, had a terrific air attack. As well as the falling bombs, hundreds of AA guns poured their tracer into the sky. The captain, First Lieutenant and I were on the bridge in a very tense state when the bridge phone rang. I answered and heard Lofty Dawson, Leading Stoker, say in an animated voice that Dixon had collapsed, crying out that he was dying, so could we send down help.

After relaying the message to the captain he told the First Lieutenant to investigate. At first the officer ignored the order. I thought he hadn't heard the order, as he failed to acknowledge it. The Captain gave him the order again, more loudly this time, but the officer again ignored it. Then, in a very loud authoritative voice, the Captain said: 'This is an order, Number One, go aft and see what is wrong there.'

The First Lieutenant gave a reply which I found appalling: 'I'm not going to traipse around the deck with all this going on,' he said. I never did discover the outcome of this non-compliance, but I do know that these two officers did not get on.

The subsequent explanation of the Dixon event was

hilarious. Apparently, after joining the Royal Navy, Dixon had gone to a fortune-teller and asked her what his chances of surviving were. She had said that if he were to see 'a shooting star pass overhead' he would die. Well, with all this tracer flying about, Dix thought: 'this is it' and had fallen down crying out thinking that he was going to die. After a drubbing by the rest of the crew he came to me to explain that it wasn't some cheap fortune-teller; in fact she had charged him half a crown.

THE SICILY LANDINGS

Obviously something was afoot with all the shipping and activity in Malta, and a few evenings later we sailed empty for Cape Passero, Sicily. Early in the morning, after a very stormy night, we went alongside the SS *Durban Castle*, a troopship carrying Canadians. As we loaded the troops from the liner's scrambling nets there was a lot of green tracer coming our way from the shoreline. However, with 200 soldiers on board we hit the beach, or thought we had. Unfortunately, a sandbar obstructed us about ten yards out and our coxswain had to wade to the beach with a rope which the soldiers then hung onto as they made their way ashore. We made a number of trips and apart from a few air attacks it wasn't a bad show.

On our last trip to the *Durban Castle* we asked their crew if they had any spare loaves of bread. They had hundreds left by their troops, so it rained loaves by the dozen from about 30 feet above us, while they had a good laugh at our expense.

I watched one of our 'monitors' bombarding the hillside and one could hear the 15-inch shells going through the air and see them bursting on the road in the hills, which was probably held by the Germans.

We left for Malta that evening, returning to Sicily a few days later to the small port of Syracuse, which was full of supply ships supporting the army just up the coast. The harbour was the subject of night attacks by enemy bombers. First they dropped flares to illuminate the harbour, then they dropped their bombs. Our task was to sail all around the port with multiple smoke canisters, the size of five-litre pots. Although they spluttered like roman candles they gave off such volumes of smoke that the port was completely covered, and even a full moon was blacked out.

One morning an Italian submarine fired a torpedo from the sea towards the entrance of the harbour. It exploded on contact with the boom net with a huge explosion and a huge column of water.

JERRY HITS THE JERRY CANS

Another morning a large merchant ship entered Syracuse and anchored about 60 yards off our port side. She had a cargo of ammunition and a deck cargo of petrol-filled jerry cans. That night she received a direct bomb hit, and just before hitting the deck I saw a huge section of the ship flying into the air. I hoped none of the debris would land on me as I lay there. Some did come very close, and a large wave broke over the bridge where I was crouching.

This was our daily routine for days until Sicily was rid of the Germans. Operation Husky, the invasion of Sicily, began 9–10 July and ended 17 August 1943. LCI (L) 111 then sailed to Augusta (see map p...). This was a larger port, which was also a seaplane base with a hangar on top of a hill.

One morning when I was washing my bed cover, four or five German FW 190 fighter-bombers flew over and dropped bombs on the Polish destroyer *Garland* and one of our monitors. These bombs were designed to explode just above the surface of the sea so as to increase their destructive power. There were a number of casualties on the ships in the harbour.

On the jetty near us a Petty Officer and able-bodied seaman were killed as they were priming a small depth charge. These charges were used every night to guard against the Italian chariot submarines which had previously caused considerable damage, crippling the battleships *Warspite* and *Queen Elizabeth* in Alexandria, Egypt and several merchant ships at Gibraltar. The latter attacks had come from an Italian depot ship in neutral Spain.

One night we were sent out to sea to escort a merchant

ship which was on fire after her cargo of coal had caught fire through internal combustion. The *Empire Moon* had been carrying the coal for a long time (apparently no one wanted it) and the cargo had self-ignited. We escorted her into Syracuse, where she was scuttled in very shallow water, and for months afterwards we would see her as we sailed by on our way to Malta.

TRIPOLI AND SALERNO

After a few weeks we sailed to Tripoli, Libya, where we anchored about a quarter of a mile from the main dockside. I used to be on the bridge all day long, as my signalman duties required. On a very hot morning I watched idly as a Landing Craft, Tank went by loaded with an unusual cargo of bits and bobs, including very large Royal Navy smoke floats, which could be thrown into the sea to create smoke screens as and when required. When the LCT was beached on the main hard of the port to unload the smoke floats ignited, sending a huge column of white smoke straight up into the sky for thousands of feet.

One of the LCT's crew, wearing sea boots and a pair of khaki shorts, was playing a hose on the float when there was a huge explosion which sent debris in all directions. One large section of steel, part of the well deck covering, whirled gently over our LCI, trailing white smoke. Unfortunately some of the debris struck other LCTs, which were loaded with jerry cans of petrol ready for our next landing at Salerno, setting them ablaze. Some were white hot down to the waterline. What caused the explosion was not known, but I suspect the heat of the sun in that month was very dangerous requiring us to keep our hosepipes on all day to cool the ship.

In September we embarked 150-170 Seychellois French-speaking troops and set sail for Palermo, Sicily. After anchoring for a day we left in the evening for Salerno. During the dusk the Seychellois troops in the well deck started a commotion. The white major in charge sent his white sergeant major down to the well deck to find out what all the excitement was about. From a small radio these troops had in their possession, they had heard that Italy had surrendered unconditionally. At the same time a message giving us that news was being flashed down the line for us to digest and flash further down the line of ships for their information.

The general feeling was that this landing would be a walkover, but it was not to be.

We arrived off the beachhead at Salerno among the fleet, which consisted of battleships, cruisers, destroyers, rocket craft, landing craft gunships, LSTs, LCTs and LCI (L)s with support aircraft. I had the communications via a loudspeaker on the bridge, where we expected to get our landing instructions. All we did get was jamming by all sorts of traffic requesting this and that and being told this and that. It was a total mess as regards the level of information conveyed by radio.

A DANGEROUS DECISION

We had been cruising among the fleet for a while when the Captain, who had been on watch all night, left the bridge, having decided to have a shower. Then the First Lieutenant decided to go wandering from the landing area to a quieter stretch of water just south. Shells started to whistle over the ship from the shore at that spot and the army major suggested to the First Lieutenant that although there was a lot of bombing and shelling going on at the beach area, it would be safer there than being the only target where we were. The Lieutenant said in an arrogant manner to the Major that when the Captain was off the bridge he was in charge, and resumed his wanderings.

I thought, 'This is not for me!' I had seen enough of the war since September without asking for trouble, so I went down to the Captain and told him what was going on. In his dressing gown he came to the bridge just as a shell screamed over. 'Ahead flank, starboard 30,' he said and as we went back to the beachhead he gave the officer a ticking of. After he had gone I had a telling off from the First Lieutenant, which I ignored. Under my breath I told what he could to himself. The impossible.

As the radio traffic was still a mess I asked the Captain

(now back on the bridge) if I could try and get through. He agreed, and I sent the following signal: 'Hello Crusader, this is ITEM 111, request we discharge our SERIAL.' The reply came back almost at once: 'Discharge SERIAL on Gold Beach.' We did this successfully alongside LCT 244, on which I saw Chick Griffiths from Brook Street, Barry. After landing our troops we hung about the beachhead all day watching the action, which included a US cruiser taking a direct shell hit and the attempts of her crew to fight the resulting fires.

A small Harbour Defence Motor Launch came around all the ships asking if there were any decorations to be awarded. We had none, so that evening we sailed back to Malta.

SHOPPING EXPEDITION

A few days later we went from Malta to Castellammare in the Bay of Naples to do some odd jobs for the army in Naples. By now we had a new First Lieutenant. He was an older man, RNVR, and he was very 'mean.'

Each day I would go ashore for the mail. The Americans had a daily newspaper called 'Stars and Stripes' and the Brits had one called the 'Union Jack'. These were priced at two lire, which was nothing as the pound was worth 400 lire. These papers were sold by an old Italian vendor on the corner of the street where I would pass by on the way to collect the mail. The First Lieutenant gave me a five-lire note to buy both papers, but as the money was worthless I gave the old vendor 50 lire. The next day the First Lieutenant gave me three lire and said to use the change from the five he had given me the day before!

Another day he ordered me to take two stokers and a few sacks and to go to Naples for supplies. Now Castellammare is at the foot of a peninsula that has Sorrento on the north side, Capri on the tip and the bay of Salerno and the port of Amalfi on the south side. Naples is about thirty or forty miles from Castellammare, where we were berthed alongside a half-built Italian cruiser which had been prematurely launched and was being used as a temporary jetty.

So the two stokers and I, with four sacks between us, had to find our own way to Naples and find potatoes, bread, tinned goods, green goods etc. and a NAAFI, all in different locations. Getting to Naples was the easy part as there was so much military traffic to-ing and fro-ing to give us a lift. Naples, however, was like Bedlam! There were white and black American GIs; French, black and white soldiers. There were Polish, New Zealanders and our own Tommies, all blocking the streets with traffic. Monte Cassino, still held by the Germans, wasn't too far away, so the city was practically the front line. What were we to do?

'Go to the Yanks' I thought. The Americans are always generous. To a motor pool I went and stupidly asked if there were any 'lorries' available. The US sergeant only understood me when I pointed to their ten-ton trucks. He was very generous and called over a six-foot plus black GI and told him to help out us 'Limeys'. That he did. Driving through the military traffic, he obtained sacks of potatoes from one place and sacks of bread from another, and all this among the most snarled-up traffic imaginable. We stopped at one o'clock and ate a half a loaf each with a tin of corned beef, and then we resumed our shopping.

The sergeant drove us back to the LCI at about six o'clock. I then went to the First Lieutenant and told him of the efforts the US driver had made on our behalf, explaining how difficult it had been, so we could give him something for all his endeavours. 'A bottle of whisky,' I thought to myself.

'Go to my canteen locker and give him a packet of ten Gold Flake cigarettes' he said. (Cost – a penny halfpenny in English money.) The Americans were used to getting cartons of American cigarettes virtually for free, and I could imagine the insult if we gave him a packet of 10 measly cigs – and English ones at that!

So I took him down to the mess deck and explained to the lads what this Yank had done for us. Out came their bottles, and after asking this huge GI whether he drank or not, we gave him an enamel US Navy grey cup with two full navy tots of rum. We all looked on in amazement as he drank it all in one gulp. After trying to splutter 'Thanks, guys,' he staggered up the ladder and we all turned out on the upper deck to see him drive off, successfully, as it happened.

NO SMOKE WITHOUT FIRE

Then we sailed around the bay of Naples, visiting the port of Torre Annunziata at the foot of Vesuvius, which was smoking a little, followed by Naples and Pozzuoli. At Naples we witnessed the population queuing for water, as the Germans had damaged the water supply before leaving the city. The main Post Office was blown up by a delayed mine, killing many civilians who were trying to communicate news of their well-being to their scattered families.

The local population was also mass doused with DDT powder to guard against typhus, which was carried by lice. I saw young and older women having a hose up their dresses to pump the DDT into their nether regions. I dined (or rather had a cup of tea and a rock cake) in the Royal Palace of King Umberto, then being used as a canteen. The cup was a bottle cut in half. There were several notices regarding the prevalence of VD and many areas were out of bounds and patrolled by Red Caps (Military Police) in Jeeps.

We eventually sailed for Malta, and at Manoel Island we were pulled out of the creek onto a metal cradle and the ship's sides and bottom were de-barnacled and de-weeded and then painted with red lead paint.

After a rather quiet Christmas we were to have sailed back to the UK. We even reached Gibraltar, but on January 14th 1944, the Big Three (Roosevelt, Churchill and Stalin) met in Morocco and laid plans for the Anzio Landings, to break the deadlock at Monte Cassino. So back we sailed to Castellammare.

On January 22nd we took on a company of British troops, members of an East Anglian regiment, and landed them at Anzio. At first the landing was quiet except for airburst shells, causing the captain to order me to put on my steel helmet. In the port an LST, 510 I think, received a direct hit as she was about to discharge her cargo of loaded lorries (trucks). Three of these trucks blew up one by one as the LST was being towed out to sea by a tug, which had tied up to the LST's stern anchor sponson.

We left for Castellammare and a few days later were joined by LCI 184. A friend of mine on board told me that the beachhead was now a siege, as the Germans had the Allied troops hemmed in and we were subject to constant shellfire and bombing. A number of British and US Navy ships had been sunk in the bay by mines and by bombs dropped from radio-controlled gliders and fighter-bombers. These gliders sank a new 10,000-ton cruiser, the *Spartan*, and a veteran destroyer, the *Inglefield*.

Action at Anzio

Of all the operations in which I participated during World War Two, in North Africa, Pantelleria, Sicily, Salerno, Anzio and Normandy, Anzio was by far the worst in terms of the amount of time in action and the variety of enemy weaponry. There were shells, mines, aircraft and radio-controlled glider bombs.

The initial landing was not so bad; apart from the occasional airburst shell it was almost peaceful. The aim of the landing was to draw the German troops from Monte Cassino, making the Allied assault on that notoriously difficult obstacle easier. The Army had to hold on to the Anzio beachhead for 14 days, whereupon the Allied Armies, having taken Monte Cassino, would link up at the beachhead and advance on Rome. However, the Germans under Field Marshal Kesselring had other ideas.

We ran about 200 troops at a time to Anzio from Naples, Pozzuoli, Castellammare and Torre Annunziata. After about a week or so, the beachhead became a siege, the Allies failing to break through at Monte Cassino and the Germans holding a tight grip on the perimeter. It was this holding scenario that was to become my worst three months of the war.

After the initial Anzio landings we loaded troops and ammunition at different ports in the Bay of Naples to supply the bridgehead. Some of the ammo was 80mm shells secured in trefoil shape.

VESUVIUS JOINS THE BOMBARDMENT

One of our supply ports was Torre Annunziata, at the foot of Vesuvius. One day the volcano erupted and covered the boat with a thick layer of grey ash. It was quite a spectacular sight, with huge columns of ash shooting into the air and lava flowing red down the side of the volcano, destroying everything in its path, not only villages but a US airfield. Our crew had to wear oilskins and steel helmets for protection until we left the port for a safer area.

This was the eruption of March 22 1944, the last major eruption of Vesuvius to date. Three villages were destroyed and great damage was done to Allied aircraft on the ground.

One of the first tastes of what was to come at Anzio was the shelling of the anchorage by a German howitzer, which fired shells weighing almost half a ton. When they landed, the huge explosion and ensuing fountain of water were stupendous. Then, interspersed with the shelling, came the air raids, either by Focke-Wulf 190 fighter bombers or medium bombers, probably Junkers 88s carrying radio-controlled bombs. Apart from the merchant ships sunk, the Royal Navy lost two cruisers and several destroyers to these attacks. Worse still happened when we were alongside the jetty at Anzio itself. There we were the main target, and on numerous occasions as we were attacked, we could actually see the bombs leaving the enemy aircraft a second before diving flat on the deck.

On one occasion, we had just arrived with a load of American GIs. As the deck of the ship was somewhat higher than the jetty, I went ashore in search of a plank of wood to assist the unloading. I'd just got ashore when a burst of ack-ack made me look up. Sure enough, there were four or five fighter-bombers diving on the ship, their bombs clearly visible as they were released. I dashed through the open door of a house and dived for the floor, only to feel the plaster ceiling coming down and the whole building shaking with the explosions.

Having decided to get out I found that dozens of GIs were trying to get in and heard myself saying 'Excuse me, excuse me.' It was useless trying to get out of course, and I had to remain in the building, hoping it would not collapse. Happily it didn't, but the navy blue overcoat I was wearing was completely ruined by the plaster and dust!

On a few occasions we were designated Guard Ship,

which meant we were in Anzio for days on end. My duty was to challenge the shipping approaching the area from the south with my signal lamp and report the ships and cargo to HQ in the ruins of the town, then send the unloading instructions to the ships concerned, using my 10-inch signal lamp. As I was both signalman and radio operator, I virtually lived on the open bridge, ready to receive signals by lamp or loudspeaker.

LAXATIVES NOT NEEDED

The loudspeaker played American popular music, almost continually, compered by a German woman, who tried to demoralise the Americans by reminding them of their families back home and the chance of their wives being unfaithful while they, the GIs, were here in Anzio. Overhead the sky was patrolled by American fighters manned by black pilots, the only such squadron throughout the whole American Air Forces. The radio programme would be interrupted by the German female propagandist, apologising for a forthcoming air raid and assuring us that the music would continue afterwards. Sure enough, the American aircraft would be lured away and over would come the Germans, bombing and strafing.

These actions and the shelling made any need for laxatives completely unnecessary! However one stoker of ours used to almost live in the bilges under the diesel engines, hoping that there would be some safety there. I used my own reasoning to help me keep my head. As the shells were travelling faster than 750 mph (roughly the speed of sound) I assumed that if I actually heard them they had already passed by, so I just looked to where they had gone, reasoning that if the shell hit you, you would not know much about it.

After a while we started to bring loads of 80mm shells to the beachhead. This I thought especially dangerous - one hit on that cargo and that would be the end of us. The unloading of these shells was carried out by black American soldiers using the 'iron fairy' (a small crane) and whenever a large shell screamed overhead they would freeze, open-eyed. One remarked to me that he'd seen a shell 'as big as a man' demolish one of the buildings alongside the jetty, and as most of the buildings had been demolished by then, I could quite believe him. A building being demolished by a large shell caused a shower of bricks and rocks to be scattered over a wide area, and the noise of them landing on the steel decks of our landing craft only served to increase one's fear of being struck.

Other memorable sights included a Flying Fortress landing in the sea and an American destroyer, hardly afloat after hitting a mine, limping back to Naples.

RETURN TO SICILY

We finally left Anzio in early April for the UK, to be ready for the Normandy landings. All in all, I feel that though we were actually hit by shellfire in Normandy later, Anzio was by far and away my worst experience during the war, for reasons I have explained.

We had sailing orders to leave the bay of Naples for Malta as the first stage of our return journey to the UK in order to prepare for the Normandy Landings. Unfortunately our main engines were in bad shape and black smoke from the diesels enveloped the boat when we had a stern wind. We had to call into Catania, Sicily, as the engines were virtually useless. The problem was with the main cylinder linings, which could not function properly because of carbon blocking the exhaust holes. The captain explained that unless we reached Malta in time we would not go home to the UK but rather stay in the Mediterranean with a few other landing craft for future landings.

All the crew got to work on the clogged linings and after about two days working flat out we managed to repair the engines just enough to make the 100 miles back to Malta, where the dockyard returned them to normal operational running. In early May we finally began our journey home.

Our first stop was Gibraltar, where we tied up alongside an LCT. I found that 'Woody' Woodward from

Tydfil Street, Barry, was a crew member on board. The captain of this vessel arranged a party the night we arrived, and Woody invited me to share corned beef pasties and beer from some huge jerry cans. The living quarters on these LCTs were terrible and they housed a huge diesel engine as well, but I had a really good time and the skipper and his tiny crew made me very welcome.

HOME WITH SOME 'RABBITS'

Our craft was leaving for the UK the next day, so Woody, who was not homeward bound, asked me to take some 'rabbits' home with me for his mother. ('Rabbit' was a naval term for presents bought abroad and destined for home.) Woody's presents were an ashtray made from molten lava from Vesuvius with an Italian silver coin bedded in its base and a big gold-coloured metal ring with the fascist symbol on it. I agreed and we set out for home that day.

As we were on our own I decided to use my bunk that night instead of catnapping draped over the parapet of the bridge as I usually did, ready to reply to any Morse challenge from other vessels. In the early hours of the morning I was sharply awakened by a seaman who said we were being challenged by an aircraft. I dashed up to the bridge just as a Coastal Command Liberator with a huge searchlight under its wing dropped a depth charge to attack us. Thankfully this missed. With my ten-inch lamp I soon identified who we were and after a few more inspections it flew off. From an aircraft I must admit that we could easily have been mistaken for a U-Boat on the surface.

We arrived at Devonport without further incident and most of the ship's company was given four days' leave in spite of the fact that all service leave had been stopped because of the pending Normandy invasion. We had been lucky, because we had been away from the UK almost two years and had participated in four major landings in the Mediterranean without mishap. When the first leave party returned it was my turn for four days' leave and I went merrily on my way.

On the second day of my leave in Barry I walked up to Tydfil Street to deliver the presents to Woody's family. I thought it odd that an older man took the gifts from me after I had explained what they were, and then just shut the door. It was not until six months later that I learned that since I had left him Woody's LCT, with three others, had foundered in a gale in the Gulf of Lyons with no survivors.

When I returned from leave to Devonport our ship had a visit from a Pilot Officer, Royal Air Force. He apologised for depth-charging us having mistaken us for a U-Boat. He said that he hadn't been quite sure, so he had dropped his depth charge wide, just in case. However, we forgave him with the usual hospitality - him a tot of rum.

We sailed from Devonport to Portsmouth and while

anchoring there I spotted a trawler which had been on the Russian convoys with us in 1941-42. We had transferred a shipmate of mine to her. Out of curiosity I called up the trawler (the *Lord Middleton*) and asked if Noble-Partridge was still on board. 'Speaking,' was the reply. There he was.

D-Day and after

The day before we sailed for the D-Day landings we and a few more Landing Craft lnfantry (Large) ships' companies were mustered in a large boat shed in Newhaven. A Royal Navy captain gave us a pep talk that went something like this:

'You men have done a great job at Pantelleria, Sicily, Salerno and Anzio and have earned the reputation of being ''the cream of the landing craft'. As such, the Admiralty has seen fit to reward you.'

This caused great speculation among the assembled crews – medals? Leave? Promotion? However all such speculation was crushed as he continued, 'You have been given the honour of landing on the extreme east flank of Sword Beach, which is expected to be the most hotly contested. I know you will conduct yourselves commensurate to the occasion.'

With that bit of information under our belts, we realised that we were in for a 'hot time', as the following account will bear out.

For this invasion we were flotilla leader and carried a Lieutenant Commander, Royal Naval Reserve, in addition to our two-ringed skipper, Harry Collinge, and a sub lieutenant, Royal Navy Volunteer Reserve, who was 'Number One'. After loading the 170 troops, we anchored in Shoreham Bay while the powers that be decided whether or not the invasion was 'on' or 'off'. The accommodation for the troops could at best be described as primitive, consisting of rows of wooden ribbed seats like park benches. It doesn't stretch the imagination to envisage what conditions were like after a few hours of being packed like sardines, with all the equipment, weapons and webbing required for landing and storming the beaches. The stench of vomit alone was terrible, most of the troops being seasick. However we duly sailed that evening. From Portsmouth we sailed to Newhaven to prepare for D-Day.

A TRIP TO THE BEACH

As dawn broke the sheer size of the operation became apparent, and it grew hour by hour. There were battleships, cruisers, destroyers and dozens of other types of craft all going south; hundreds of all types of ships with one purpose – to land and support an army in Normandy.

Through the ring of bombarding vessels we sailed, and as the beach grew nearer one could see splashes as shells and mortars homed in on and near the landing area. As we reached the beach and began unloading, the first casualties were sustained (orders were for all wounded to be landed on the beach). There was one soldier being helped by two others, his left foot and boot as one in a mangle of flesh and leather. I shall never forget the almost apologetic look he gave me as he passed by.

An LCT shot alongside us and on to the beach with its cargo of tanks ablaze and ammunition exploding. Able Seaman Harry Gee, a Yorkshireman, was on our forecastle blazing away with his Oerlikon 20mm cannon – a brave effort, bearing in mind that the air was alive with bullets and shrapnel etc. On the upper deck I was observing the landing with great interest, when all hell broke loose.

As I ducked back into the wireless office for cover, we sustained a direct hit. The usual smell of cordite and the cries of wounded men came from No. 3 troop space, where a shell had entered the packed space and exploded, leaving wounded and dying men as the shrapnel made its exit from the port to the starboard side.

Our skipper shouted down the voice pipe for me to see if No. 3 troop space was cleared. This I did with great alacrity, as I knew from past experience that as soon as we had disembarked all our troops, we could kedge (anchor) off the beach and reach the relative quiet among the offshore fleet. However, as I was halfway down the ladder of No. 2 troop space, a soldier who was sitting on the bench with his back to me turned and said, 'Come and help my mate, Jack.' I replied, 'You had better get off quick mate, all the rest have landed'. He replied, 'I can't – my leg has had it – help my mate.'

The water was pouring in, and although not deep as such it became a hazard to wounded troops, who were in danger of drowning as well as making their injuries worse when the ship was rolling. As I came to the soldier who had called out I saw that his leg was hanging off below the knee, so I opened the tin of morphia ampoules and jabbed one into his thigh with the attached needle. Turning to his mate, who was semi-conscious, I undid his webbing and tried to sit him on the seat next to his wounded mate. He was a big chap and his gas mask kept catching under the seat. I said: 'Try and help yourself, mate,' but all I got was a vague, incoherent mumbling.

AMPUTATION WITH A BREAD-KNIFE

I finally got him seated and saw that both his legs were shattered below the knees, so I jabbed a needle of morphine into each of his thighs. These flat tins of morphia contained 6 to 8 ampoules each, with needles attached which could be used by removing the cap from the needle and then squeezing the drug into the casualty. Then I took a breadknife from the galley and sawed off the leg of the first soldier. The part of his leg below the knee was hanging off and moving to and fro in the water as the ship rolled.

By now, some other crew members had arrived in the troop space and the task of getting the dead and wounded up to the deck above began. One soldier looked all right at first, but a closer look revealed a hole of about one inch in diameter behind his ear. He just sat dribbling in a semi haze. The total extent of his injury wasn't known. He, the dead and the rest of the casualties were later put aboard a destroyer, which carried a medical officer. We had only one wire stretcher, so most of the wounded were carried up the ladder by way of one man supporting the shoulders with his hands under the arms and one man supporting the legs. Not the most satisfactory way of handling wounded men.

One of the men I was helping must have had internal injuries, for his face was a leaden colour and he just sighed and gave up the ghost as we reached the top of the ladder.

The skipper had told us to try to comfort the wounded as best we could, but just what can one say or do under those circumstances? It was a mercy that we found a destroyer with medical facilities aboard in very short time. The dead and wounded were placed all along a narrow passage on the port side and the wounded were kept as comfortable as was humanly possible.

After passing all the dead and wounded to the destroyer, we sailed directly back to Newhaven. When the tide went out, we were left high and dry on what was called a 'gridiron', a wooden platform on the bed of the harbour.

Some workmen from the Southern Railway pumped us out and welded dozens of patches of shell damage in a very short time.

That night we were loaded again, and thus began what was to be a daily shuttle to the beachhead, the only respite being riding out of the famous five-day storm, which caused severe damage to all the unloading facilities.

We dried out on the beach one day and had to switch off all the electrics. I was down below when I heard a loud explosion. As I came up on deck I was aware of debris falling all around. At first I thought we were under shellfire once again but it was the army blowing up wrecks!

I should mention that as well as being the telegraphist I was also the signalman, which served me in good stead as a witness to all the landings in which we took part, including all the Mediterranean landings. Anzio was particularly rough, thanks to the constant air attacks and shelling, but I must record my admiration at the courage and fortitude of the British tommy. At Anzio, I expressed these feelings to a particularly brave soldier. He turned to me and said 'Jack, let me tell you something, I couldn't get off that tin box ship of yours quick enough.' Horses for courses?

Once while beached on 'Sword' Beach I experienced some apprehension as hundreds of aircraft began approaching from inland with multiple ack-ack bursts. Thankfully the aircraft were ours and the ack-ack was German.

After beaching we were caught up in the June 1944 storm and witnessed the destruction of much of the Mulberry Harbour.

Back to Italy, and the Greek problem

In August 1944 I was drafted to HMS *Westcliff*, a Combined Operation barracks near Southend-on-Sea. This barracks consisted of streets of houses which had been barbed-wired off. They were named Blackfriars Street, Whitefriars Street etc. Until December 1944 we were under continuous attack by V1s and V2s. A V2 rocket hit the entrance of the Southend Pier a few hundred yards away.

In December I was on my way back to Italy on an old liner arriving at Naples on Christmas Day. For a few days I was billeted in Fort Del Ova, a fortification overlooking the bay and port of Naples. About six of us were put in an old cell using iron hooks set in walls for our hammocks.

One evening we saw a very creepy film called the *The Uninvited*, with Ray Milland. It was so scary that none of us six grown-up sailors would sleep in our cells that night.

A few days later I was put on a train and travelled over the mountains to Taranto on the Adriatic coast. The carriage had no glass in the windows and snow filled up the compartment. Early next morning an able-bodied seaman and I were put in a large barracks in the naval base. There were only two of us in this huge empty building and we were without the usual facilities such as hot water or central heating. To shower we would wash under the shower nozzle to get wet, dash out and soap ourselves and then dash back under the cold water to wash off the soap before drying ourselves.

AROUND THE ADRIATIC

After a few days I went by truck to Bari. What a change! Earlier in the war when I had visited the port for a cup of tea I used to mount wooden steps fixed to the jetty above the hundreds of 1000lb bombs. There used to be a cafe there. This jetty or mole was the landing and storage place for the US Army Air Force based at Foggia. Now in 1945 there was no mole, but there were the remains of a US Liberty ship with its four-inch gun pointing out of the water towards the land. This Liberty, its entire cargo and the thousands of bombs on the mole had blown up, killing hundreds of civilians as well as Allied servicemen.

From Bari we moved, as the war was ending, to several ports on the Adriatic Sea. At Ancona we found two things of note. An LCI was in dry dock with its flat keel turned up like the sole of a shoe after she had struck a mine. The other was a dockside 'arena.' This consisted of hundreds of baulks of timber and was about 20 feet long. Along the side of the arena there were thousands of rats forming a court. With several of the ship's company we bombarded the rats with steel nuts and bolts, which caused them to scatter and disappear. Other Adriatic ports we visited were Venice, Trieste, Zara, Pola, Fiume, Sibenic and Split.

THE EXILED GREEKS

In August 1945 while in back in Malta with LC(I) 161, I was exchanged for a telegraphist who was HO (Hostilities Only) serving on the Landing Craft Infantry 252. He was due to be demobbed, so I, as a general service rating with about eight years on my 12-year contract still to run, was the obvious choice to replace him. I was on my twentieth month of serving in the Mediterranean at this time.

The next day LC(I) 161 and LC(I) 252 left Sliema Creek. We turned to starboard heading for Greece and my former craft turned to port heading for Old Blighty.

When we arrived in Piraeus a few days later, we received two pieces of information. First, there was a civil war in progress and, second, the drachma was about 130 to the pound. Altogether we had four missions to accomplish while we were there.

The first was to take Greek families back to the Greek islands, as many had been in exile on account of the war.

It was very enjoyable taking all the families with their furniture to the various islands, concluding with Rhodes. The sad part was taking some Italian families from Rhodes back to Italy.

Rhodes was taken from the Turks after WWI because the Turks had chosen to fight on the side of the Germans, who had lost, so it was given to Italy, who had sided with Britain and France. However, in WWII the situation was reversed. Italy had allied itself with Germany, so Rhodes was given to Greece, which had been on the side of the Allies. I don't know why these Italian families had had to leave and go to Italy, but it was a sad event.

The second mission was to Suda Bay in Crete, where a memorial service was to be held for the New Zealand troops who had died in battle in June 1941. The RN cruiser *Ajax* brought New Zealand's General Freyberg and a naval squad with rifles to address the service, and we had the job of ferrying the General, the Captain of HMS *Ajax* and the firing party from *Ajax* to the jetty near the site of the service. Also in Suda Bay was the wreck of HMS *York*, an eight-inch cruiser, which had been sunk there in 1941. I remembered HMS *York* paying a courtesy call to Barry in 1933 when as a young lad I had gawped at this beautiful grey-painted monster warship along with hundreds of other Barrians.

Our third task was to sail to Tobruk in North Africa to bring back to Piraeus a few hundred Greek sailors who had been arrested and imprisoned by the British for mutiny in the Egyptian port of Alexandria in 1942. Then in 1945 we were taking them back to Greece for further imprisonment, this time by the Greeks themselves. We completed two of these missions in a month. Why the Greek sailors had mutinied in the first place I had no idea nor do I know what happened to them back in the home country.

TYRE TROUBLE IN TOBRUK

Greece had been occupied by the Germans for four years. As said before, on our arrival in Piraeus there were 130 drachma to the pound. Within a few months it had gone up to 2000, then 20,000. As getting paid by the Royal Navy in drachma was a gamble, we decided to use our own initiative. For instance, while in Tobruk we had picked up some tyres that had been left behind by the Eighth Army. At first we used them as ship's fenders but when we arrived back in port we sold them for a large bundle of drachma, which we shared around the mess.

The next time we went to Tobruk, realising the value of these tyres, we put fenders all along both sides of the ship! Unfortunately a naval commander walked by our vessel and demanded to know from the Captain why there were so many. The Captain answered that obviously they were for the protection of the ship's sides, being fenders. The Commander replied sarcastically that we were a small

LCL(I) and not the *Queen Mary*, then he made us take them from the side and throw them into the harbour. We did this with regret, but after this fussy naval officer had left we salvaged a good number of them and sold them the instant we got back to Piraeus for drachma notes - these were not counted but measured in inch-thick piles for distribution. Although they were useless for buying anything or exchanging, decent wine, women and song had a payday.

One of our seamen was very closely connected to a Greek girl who was always present when we left harbour and returned. When we were about to leave Greece for the last time I have never seen such a scene of lamentation! She was screaming and scrabbling on the ground amid dust and gravel with all her family. I don't know exactly what had been promised or how far the relationship had developed, but the parting was something to behold.

SHIPSHAPE AND MALTA FASHION

Arriving back at Malta we had to pass Fort St Angelo, the Commander in Chief Mediterranean's HQ. All his staff were dressed in immaculate white and were present to stand to attention while their bugler blew the salute to which we were entitled, as a naval vessel entering harbour. I could imagine the disgust felt by these nicely-attired staff when they had to salute this rusty craft with its khaki-dressed sailors as it sailed by to Mersa Creek.

We had not switched off our engines when a staff car pulled up and a captain boarded our landing craft. He tried to criticise our skipper about the state of the vessel. This was 1946, the war was over and our Captain was waiting to be demobbed. He told the naval captain a few home truths. For a start, to make our craft to look smart we needed paint, cloths and scrubbing brushes, which were apparently reserved for the peacetime Mediterranean fleet, and unless he got these materials the landing LCI would remain looking like a rust bucket. The captain stormed off in his nice white naval dress.

A little later he returned with a naval party loaded with all the cleaning and painting materials required, plus our sailing orders – to head for a remote part of Gozo and we not to return to the Grand Harbour until we were fit to be saluted by the Commander–in–Chief. So off we went to a small cove with a sandy beach about twelve yards wide at a remote part of the island of Gozo. Everyone worked in the morning to get the ship up to scratch. We then slept or swam the rest of the day. After a few weeks of this we looked prim and proper and were ready to return to Sliema Creek.

We then joined a Landing Ship Tank, a large double-decker tank-landing craft with Royal Naval Reserve officers. These men were experienced merchant navy officers who had joined the Naval Reserve before the war. Our captain was from my hometown of Barry; his name was Hughes as I remember. At times he would talk about the Linnets, the Barry Town football club. For the first and only time I had my own cabin.

One job took us to Trieste in the Adriatic where we had to take on Surrendered Enemy Personnel – Germans who were to ditch over the side of the ship into the Adriatic tons of bombs and shells which were no longer needed.

A Court Martial and a cutlass

In 1946/47, while waiting for my next posting, I was based on Manoel Island, Sliema, Malta. As the war had been over for some time, the number of navy personnel on the island had been much reduced.

One day I was summoned to see a Chief Petty Officer who informed me that I was now in charge of a prisoner who was in the cells awaiting court martial. This meant escorting the prisoner to and fro for meals and making sure of his presence in the cells at nine in the evening for the officer of the watch's inspection.

He was a nice chap, a stoker who had deserted to marry a local Maltese girl but had been captured by a Maltese policeman working for the Royal Navy. For a few days I would let him out of the cells for a few hours so that he could see his wife-to-be, in return for a promise that he would be back for the officer's inspection at nine o'clock.

When the day of the court martial arrived I was belted

up and put in charge of two stokers to take the prisoner to HMS *Wolfe*, a submarine depot ship, where the trial was to take place. Arriving on a half-ton truck at the *Wolfe* at Msida Creek, my party and I disembarked and looked for a reception committee. However there was none. We hung around for a while wondering what to do. The prisoner gave us some gum that his girlfriends had given him. We thanked him and proceeded to chew it. Then we boarded the *Wolfe* via one of the gangways.

On deck and still wondering what to do and where to go, a somewhat officious voice came from the deck above demanding to know who was in charge. Lifting my eyes up, I saw a very severe-looking Royal Navy captain who asked whether we were chewing gum. After a confirmative reply his face coloured up, and he said in an explosive voice: 'Spit the filthy stuff over the side! I won't have gum on my ship!' He then stalked off, leaving us still none the wiser as to what we should do.

I proceeded to ask a few members of the crew the whereabouts of the ship's Regulating Office, and after much searching I finally found it. I was then issued with a belt and sheathed cutlass and directed to the captain's cabin where the court martial was to be held. Incidentally, this cutlass was so long that it touched the ground as I walked, the metal scabbard making a loud clanging noise.

On reaching the Captain's cabin I waited outside until a voice from within ordered: 'Enter the prisoner!' I called the escort to attention, opened the cabin door and walked in, only to be pushed back into the passage, prisoner and escort too, by an irate Royal Navy captain from the Secretariat Department, who was going to take charge of the trial proceedings. He explained that next time the order was given only the prisoner and I must enter. I would be behind the prisoner with the cutlass unsheathed and held upright in front of me.

This I did, and entered the huge cabin. On my left was a desk on which sat a lieutenant who was to be the prisoner's counsel. On my right was a row of seats behind a dock for the Maltese constable who was to be the chief witness. The row behind was for the audience. Alongside the dock were four chairs and a desk for the four Royal Navy captains who were to adjudicate.

The trial went on and I swear that the defendant did not have a clue as to what it was all about, but he pleaded guilty anyhow. He and I were standing in front of two chairs during the trial and I can tell you that the cutlass grew heavier by the minute and we were not allowed to sit on the chairs.

The trial over, I marched the prisoner out of the cabin. To my relief a gunnery Petty Officer took over, so I wearily walked back to Manoel Island. I was late for dinner, but the CPO had arranged for the cook to make me something special to go with my tot of neat rum.

For what it's worth I did hear that the prisoner was

found guilty of desertion and was given two years in Exeter jail, then a discharge from the Royal Navy.

Bartering and black markets

In late November 1947, I read an Admiralty Fleet Order stating that some hundreds of thousands of pounds had been donated to the Royal Navy Benevolent Trust charity. This was money unclaimed by navy personnel who had served in the Mediterranean from early 1943 to late 1947. As I wasn't informed of this benefit before the giveaway I received nothing. Here's how I had coped with the worthless toilet paper 'Money of the Med.'

While sailing off the coasts of North Africa, Italy and Greece one had to cope with being paid in lire, drachma and British Military Authority money, which had as little value as toilet paper. I would make something of this worthless money by selling my cigarette ration on the black market or by only drawing my 'casual' payment, the minimum the navy stipulated to ensure that our ablutions were taken care of.

In 1945 when based at Barletta on the east coast of Italy, we were tasked to take Marshal Tito's partisans across the Adriatic through minefields to where we hoped to land them in Yugoslavia. One morning at Pay Parade the new, green sub-lieutenant asked me how much of my week's pay I wanted. I stated the minimum amount allowed, which caused the First Lieutenant to say that he could not credit how I could spend a damn sight more than him with a 'casual,' when he as a First Lieutenant could spend all his month's pay on a solitary visit to the opera house to see the Polish Ballet.

I was honest, and told him point blank that I sold my cig ration on the black market. He was aghast, and told me I was risking my career by these illegal practices. I replied 'Since 1939 I have been happy to be still alive when I wake up each morning.' He made no comment, so I said to him: 'As you don't smoke, why don't you let me sell your cigarette rations?'

He wouldn't give consent to that so I said: 'Well, sir, if I find loose cigarettes in the chart and radio room, whoever has left the articles will later find quite a good profit under the Admiralty charts. It's trading, really.'

I forgot all about the matter for a few days, but a little while later I found two month's cigarette ration on my radio desk. It was obvious who the owner of this 'lost' property, was so I sold the property. I kept my 50% 'commission' and left the lire under the Admiralty charts on the table.

I returned to the radio room a little later to find the

First Lieutenant pretending to update the charts. He suddenly put his pencil down and turned over the charts, exposing the trading money. 'It is too much,' he said. He gave half of it back, so I was 75% up on the deal. From then on the trading became regular - sometimes cigarettes, sometimes shoes or canteen goods.

BURBERRYS AND BULLETS

One morning I found a nicely folded-up new Burberry raincoat on my desk, which I assumed belonged to the First Lieutenant. I promptly sold it in the cafe at the end of the jetty. To my horror, when I returned to the chart room the captain was looking for his Burberry. I ran back to the café and immediately tried to buy it back, but they refused. I went back to the LCI and took out the quartermaster's automatic pistol. Having removed the magazine, I rushed back to the café, but they still refused to sell back the coat.

I did not realise that there was still a round in the chamber. The pistol went off and the bullet ended up in the wall of the cafe. This did the trick, and the Burberry was returned to me post-haste.

Back I went to the wardroom with the item and returned it to the captain.

'Where did you find it?'

I replied: 'Behind my wireless set, sir.'

The skipper shot me a warning look, so this closed the trading business in Italy for the time being. The Captain knew what was going on, but the war was almost over and he was only in for the duration, so he was not too fussed about what crew members were getting up to as long as the LCI was operated efficiently.

We were successful in our nightly trips to Yugoslavia, although some motor launches with 20mm cannons were unlucky and met German flak ships. Upon their return blood was visible on the decks.

POSTSCRIPT

After four years in the Mediterranean, the navy allowed me back to the UK for a few months before they sent me away to a major wireless station which was situated on the 13.5 milestone on the Bukit Tima Road outside the city of Singapore. This wireless station in the wilderness was known as Kranji, and consisted of a selection of Nissen huts and a few admin buildings. Serving in this isolated spot was like being in a monastery.

However, after a few years I duly returned to HMS *Drake* at Devonport and was awarded a twelve-month petty officers' course in Portsmouth. After successfully passing this course I was drafted to the frigate HMS *Loch Insh*, which was the flagship of the Sixth Frigate Flotilla and was commanded by Captain Roy Foster-Brown.

The main object of interest aboard *Loch Insh* was the discovery of the wreck of the missing submarine, HMS *Affray*. She had been missing for a few weeks. A thorough search by a fleet of vessels led by *Loch Insh* led to the *Affray* being discovered in a deep trough called the Hard Deep off the Channel Islands.

After a year on the *Loch Insh* I was put in charge of radio communications on board HMS *Termagant*, a converted destroyer-cum-frigate. We exercised with submarines off the Isle of Bute for twelve months, returning after each daily exercise at nightfall to the bay off Rothesay.

In February 1954 I was finally discharged from the navy after finishing my fourteen and a half years. Upon reflection, I feel that I was exceptionally fortunate to have survived and to have benefited from such a variety of experiences.

Landing Craft Infantry

The Landing Craft, Infantry or LCI were several classes of sea-going amphibious assault ships of the Second World War utilized to land large numbers of infantry directly onto beaches. They were developed in response to a British request for a vessel capable of carrying and landing substantially more troops than the wooden Landing Craft Assault (LCA). The result was a small steel ship that could land 200 troops, travelling from rear bases on its own bottom at a speed of up to 17 knots. Some 923 were built starting in 1943, serving in both the Pacific and European theaters, including a number that were converted into heavily armed beach assault support ships. Commonly called 'Elsie Items,' the LCI filled a niche between the small LCAs and the larger Landing Ship Tank (LST).

DEVELOPMENT

In 1942 the British concluded that a larger landing craft was needed than the LCA, which could carry only 35 troops to the shore. This would carry 200 troops at up to 17 knots and be as capable at landing as the LCA. Since a steel hull would be needed and steel was already earmarked for building destroyers at home, the US was approached. There the plans were developed into the LCI (L) - Landing Craft Infantry (Large).

The hull of the LCI (L) was relatively long and narrow. The deck was wider than the prow and two gangways on either side gave onto a pair of ramps that were lowered, and down which troops would disembark.

SERVICE HISTORY

The first LCI(L)s entered service in 1943, chiefly with the Royal Navy (RN) and United States Navy. Early models were capable of carrying 180 troops; this was increased to 210 later. Craft in service with the two navies had some variation according to national preferences. Some 923 LCI were built in ten American shipyards and 211 provided under lend-lease to the Royal Navy. In Royal Navy service they were known as 'HM LCI (L)-(pennant number)'.

http://reference.findtarget.com/search/Landing%20Craft%20Infantry/

Navsource Online: Amphibious Photo Archive

HM LCI (L) 111

LCI (L) 111 was transferred to the United Kingdom for the duration of World War 2

LCI – 1 Class Landing Craft Infantry (Large):

Laid down in 1942, location unknown

Launched in 1942

Delivered under terms of the Lend-Lease Act to the United Kingdom, 22 December 1942, commissioned HM LCI (L) -111

Returned to US Naval custody, and struck from the Naval Register, 27 March 1946

Final Disposition, sold by the Maritime Commission, 17 February 1948, fate unknown

SPECIFICATIONS

Displacement 216 t.(light), 234 t.(landing), 389 t.(loaded)

Length 158' 5½'

Beam 23' 3'

Draft Light, 3'1½' mean, Landing, 2' 8' forward, 4' 10' aft, Loaded, 5' 4' forward, 5' 11' aft

Speed 16 knots (max.), 14 knots maximum continuous

Complement 3 officers, 21 enlisted

Troop capacity 6 Officers, 182 enlisted

Cargo capacity 75 tons

Armor 2' plastic splinter protection on gun turrets, conning tower and pilot house

Endurance 4000 miles at 12 knots, loaded, 500 miles at 15 knots; and 110 tons of fuel

Armament: four single 20mm guns, one forward, one amidships, two aft, later added two .50 cal machine guns

Fuel capacity 130 tons, lube oil 200 gal.

Propulsion: two sets of 4 GM diesels, 4 per shaft, BHP 1,600, twin variable pitch propellers

http://www.navsource.org/archives/10/15/150111.htm